No Hurdle Too High

No Hurdle Too High

The Story of Show Jumper Margie Goldstein Engle

Mona Pastroff Goldstein

Writer's Showcase
San Jose   New York   Lincoln   Shanghai

No Hurdle Too High
The Story of Show Jumper Margie Goldstein Engle

Writer's Showcase
an imprint of iUniverse.com, Inc.

For information address:
iUniverse.com, Inc.
5220 S 16th, Ste. 200
Lincoln, NE 68512
www.iuniverse.com

Cover Photograph Copyright © 2000 Charles Mann

ISBN: 0-595-18337-9

Printed in the United States of America

Dedication

To people everywhere who pursue their dreams.
The future belongs to those who believe in the beauty of their dreams.

Eleanor Roosevelt

Epigraph

The future belongs to those who believe in the beauty of their dreams.
Eleanor Roosevelt

Contents

Chapter One

At the first AGA Grand Prix of the new year, 1997, we meet Margie Goldstein Engle and watch her winning the Rider of the Year competition for the fifth time. There would be more AGA yearly awards in the future, but none so exciting as this one.

Chapter Two

From birth to pre-school, these years reveal the learning of persistence while trying to win acceptance from her older brothers.

Chapter Three

Life with Margie is like living in a zoo!

Chapter Four

Margie meets friends, her "first love," and gains the skills and pleasure from both.

List of Illustrations

Charles Mann's Cover Photograph: Margie and Hidden Creek's Perin during Olympic Trials.

Foreword

I can still remember that day as if it were only yesterday. The year was 1984; the occasion, the Individual Show Jumping Finals at the summer Olympic Games. A fellow junior rider and I sat huddled in front of my television set, immersed in the glory of our onscreen heroes. The U.S. team—Leslie Burr and *Albany*, Joe Fargis and *Touch of Class*, Conrad Homfeld and *Abdullah*, and Melanie Smith and *Calypso*—appeared larger than life, clearing tremendous obstacles with power and grace. Having already clinched team gold, the riders now vied for individual medals.

I had my own personal favorite—Fargis' mount, *Touch of Class*. The bay mare—a thoroughbred off the track—was the smallest of the equine athletes. At just over 15 hands, the odds seemed stacked against victory for the little mare. But what this small horse lacked in size, she made up for in courage and strength. And, to my amazement, she cleared each obstacle, becoming only the second U.S. show jumper in history to win the individual Olympic gold medal.

What is it that makes certain athletes excel against the odds? When talent is equal—such as in the Olympic Games—what sets a true champion apart from the rest? Is it luck, or fate, or simple destiny? I believe, in fact, that it comes down to pure inner strength—a feeling that nothing is insurmountable.

To me, there is no better example of such fortitude than show jumper Margie Goldstein Engle. From the time she began taking lessons while still a young child, Margie's talent was extraordinary. The youngster had a natural ability to school even the most difficult horses. But, even then,

Margie had so much more than talent; her courage propelled her toward success.

Of course, there were many setbacks along the way. Unable to afford a horse of her own, young Margie rode any mount that was offered to her—stoppers, green ponies, and those that frightened more experienced riders. In order to earn extra lessons, she mucked stalls and performed a variety of daily barn chores. As a teen, she taught the younger students and drove a truck and trailer to various horse shows. It wasn't always easy, but Margie persevered. She continued this hectic schedule right on through college, where she maintained an impressive 4.0 average.

Like many riders, Margie sustained a series of injuries, yet she never let such accidents hinder her focus. Trainers told her that she was too small to ride jumpers, but Margie held on tight to her dream. She always put the best interests of her animals first, and never made excuses for her own mistakes. And despite setbacks that included missing two consecutive Olympic trials due to injury, Margie never gave up on her dream of one day competing at the Olympic Games. She achieved that goal in 2000, placing 10th upon Mike Polaski's young horse, Perin.

Margie has achieved incredible success thus far in her career. She has set numerous records and is a bona fide "superstar" in the equestrian world. Yet, through it all, she has remained humble. Despite her hectic schedule, she is never too busy to chat with friends or sign autographs for awestruck junior riders.

Each and every one of us has a dream. Deep inside, we all aspire to do great things, to test ourselves to the highest peak. We may keep our dreams to ourselves, afraid that others may laugh at us. Or we may share them for an outward goal—winning an equitation final, perhaps, or placing well in a certain competition.

Perhaps you have a lofty dream yourself—to win at the Finals or to one day compete for the USET. Or perhaps your dream is a much simpler one—to clear a three-foot, six- inch oxer, to nail each distance on a small hunter course, or simply to master a flying lead change. Whatever your dream, whatever your level, you'll undoubtedly enjoy *No Hurdle Too High*. For Margie Goldstein Engle proves to us that with courage, determination, and sheer hard work, there is no "hurdle" high enough to prevent you from obtaining your goal.

Kimberly Gatto

Author, Michelle Kwan: Champion on Ice
and An Apple A Day: A Heartwarming Collection of True Horse Stories

Acknowledgements

For their patience and guidance, I would like to thank and acknowledge the National Writers Association of South Florida. The critique group, of which I was a member, offered me helpful and insightful suggestions.

My education was further enhanced when two giants in the field of show jumping, Frank Chapot and William Steinkraus, encouraged and directed my efforts to Elizabeth Carnes, the publisher/owner of Half Halt Press, Incorporated. Beth not only read the manuscript, but sent it to freelance writer, Kimberly Gatto, for review. Kim, the author of *Michelle Kwan: Champion on Ice* and *An Apple A Day*, is also an accomplished equestrienne. Her knowledgeable suggestions to me, a non-rider, made me aware of the unique features and required preparation of the sport. She continues to be extremely supportive and helpful.

Winona Sullivan, author of the Sister Cecile mystery series, teaches and guides with a deft, knowledgeable style, zeroing in on the details that make a story come to life. I am fortunate to be in her class.

Without my family, there would be no book. They provided the events, of course. But, more than that, each offered direct assistance. My husband, Irv, can spot a misspelled word at twenty feet away. Surely, he could have made a career as a proofreader if needed. Margie provided me with time, of which she has little, and background, of which she has much. Her husband, Steve, and my grandson, Jeff, served admirably as computer consultants. My older grandson, Matthew, an accomplished fiction writer, reviewed and critiqued the final results.

The choice of a cover photograph was never in doubt once we saw the beautiful picture of Margie and Hidden Creek's Perin, taken by Charles

Mann of Adelphi, Maryland. He captured the resolve of both athletes as they began their pursuit to represent the United States in the 2000 Olympic Trials. Both Mr. Mann and I have pledged photographer and author book profits to the United States Equestrian Teams (USET).

Rifka Keilson of iUniverse provided both information and patience in enormous quantities.

To one and all I offer thanks and appreciation.   M.P.G.

Chapter One

Introduction to the Show Jumping World

Every Sunday afternoon for the first two months of the year, we leave our home in Miami, point our car north, and drive to the Winter Equestrian Festival in Palm Beach.

"Hurry, Irv, hurry. We'll miss the riders walking the course."

"Easy does it, Mona. Let's see if we have everything."

My methodical husband could not be rushed. He looked around the car. "Okay, we have our sun glasses, our hats. We'll get the programs at the gate. I'll put these papers for Margie in the trunk until after the show."

I shifted from one foot to the other. On this crisp, cool afternoon in February, 1997, the sun's warm, soothing rays almost succeeded in banishing the anxiety I always felt before one of our daughter's horse shows.

We headed toward the opening of the Palm Beach Equestrian Center, maneuvering our way through hordes of children, adults, and an assortment of Jack Russell terriers, dachshunds, and other well-cared-for dogs.

"They sure do love their animals," I said to Irv. "It looks as much like a dog show as a horse one."

The voices of several announcers from different areas blurred together as we walked toward the international arena. The smells of grilling meats, soft pretzels, and pungent fruits floated on the gentle breeze. We walked around the bright yellow-and-white striped tents and worked our way to the west-side bleachers, anticipating and hoping to avoid the intensity of the later sun.

"Mrs. Goldstein, Mr. Goldstein, over here, over here." We looked around to see where the voice called from and saw Margie's friend pointing to the seats she had saved for us. Most of the spectators were already seated, but some stood in friendly clusters, chatting excitedly about the equestrian show-jumping event awaiting us.

"I'm so proud of Margie," said Nancy. "Here we are at the largest and most important Grand Prix in the country this year, and Marge is going to break records today."

I reached out and hugged my daughter's loyal friend, "Please, God, let that be the *only* thing she breaks! Oh, Nancy, let's talk about something— *anything*—else. Doesn't the field look beautiful?"

The spacious emerald green arena glowed with potted plants and flowers next to colorful hurdles, carefully designed to please the crowd and distract the horses. The multi-colored sponsors' emblems vied with the bright yellow, red, orange, and purple bouquets that accented most of the jumps. Bushy olive-colored raffia palms waved gently by the sides of the wide black-and-white striped oxers. By the Seaquarium obstacle, plastic dolphins stood ready to leap. The bleachers in front of the airy tents bustled with activity from the excited fans, anxious to watch the final 1996 American Grand Prix (AGA) competition and see the presentation of the AGA Rider of the Year Award.

Irv spied Margie's childhood riding instructor and called out, "Hey, Karen, come join us."

"From the looks of things, I got here just in time. I see they must have posted the course design."

Suddenly, groups of men and women, wearing red or black jackets, streamed into the arena. Only those who had earned the honor of representing the United States Equestrian Team (USET) could wear red. The riders strode purposefully: walking the field, checking out the hurdles, noting the distance between them, and mentally converting their own steps to the number of horse strides needed to position their steeds for each lift off. This walk-through introduced the rider to the day's specific course. Their horses would see it for the first time when the class began.

"Which one is Margie?" asked one of Nancy's riding pupils.

"Look for the smallest one," she replied. She then turned to me. "Remember when the professionals told her she'd never make it in the world of show jumping? They told her she was much too little to control all that brute power."

"I remember they wanted her to be a jockey, but you know our gal. The more they told her she couldn't reach Grand Prix level, the more determined she became."

We quickly located her petite form, watched her pace off the strides, and laughed as she stretched her legs as far as they would extend.

I turned to my husband and said, "Do you realize what those thirty riders out there represent? Many of them are her childhood heroes. There are Olympians with gold and silver medals, World Cup contenders, Nation's Cup winners—that's quite a group!"

Irv responded, "Well, Mona, Margie's the only one out there who has ever been Rider of the Year four times. You don't have to worry about her credentials."

"It's her *body* I worry about. I'll be glad when this is over and she's safe!"

We were in for a long wait. Margie and the other twenty-nine American participants had earned their standings after a year of intense competition. They would ride in reverse order; and, because of her high ranking, she was scheduled to ride next-to-last. The winner of last year's class, Laura Chapot, would ride last.

When the competition began, we watched each horse and rider combination. They were beautiful to observe—strong, graceful, and skilled. But the course designer from Bolivia, Jose Pepe Gamarra, had done his job too well, judging by what followed. Pepe, knowing that he was dealing with top riders and scopey horses, those with natural athletic ability, filled the large field with difficult obstacles. To complete the thirteen numbered jumps and combinations, sixteen jumping efforts in all, the riders would have to make many sharp turns to stay within the time limit of ninety-two seconds. Particularly challenging were both the number eight triple-combination and the number twelve double-combination. Also, the space between the two fences of each oxer measured over five feet, so that the horses would not only have to clear the heights, but stretch out to clear the widths. There was nothing easy on this field! Every rail knocked down at any obstacle or every hoof in the water or on the tape of the water jump would add four faults to many riders' scores.

The talented Anne Kurrsinski, who had recently won the Team Silver Medal at the 1996 Olympics, as well as Medals in two previous Olympics, rode third. The tricky space within the triple caused her horse, Suddenly, to knock down the top rails on both the 8*a* and 8*b* fences for a total of eight penalty faults. The efforts continued, but no one rode fault free. At mid-way in the competition, two riders had four faults, which placed them in the lead.

Fellow 1996 Olympic winner, Peter Leone, galloped onto the field. His strong, solid showing through the triple thrilled the spectators. Just as he rode from 12a to 12b, Crown Royal Let's Go took a small half stride before jumping the second half of the combination. His hoof hit the fence and it thudded to the ground.

Next came McLain Ward, the 1991 Rookie of the Year, atop Orchestra. The breathless announcer cheered the first clear round, but then added,

"Two seconds over the time allowed. There will be a half-point time fault." McLain was now out in front.

The thrilling duo, Michael Matz and Rhum IV, entered the fray, and the spectators roared in anticipation. Michael had not only won the 1996 Team Silver for the United States in Atlanta, but he had been selected to lead the U.S. delegation and carry our flag for the final victory parade. This unassuming hero, who had risked his life rescuing passengers from an airline crash only a few years prior, rode beautifully. Rhum's hoof hit the last fence of the triple. It rocked in the cup, but it did not fall. They approached the number ten hurdle, painted brown to blend easily with the earth below. Rhum hit the top rail with his front legs and the sound of its falling seemed to echo throughout the arena. Michael joined the group of eight riders with four faults.

Margie and Hidden Creek's Laurel, a beautiful dark-bay (brown), Dutch-bred mare, entered the ring. While the loud speaker introduced them, they walked slowly past the most colorful and distracting hurdles. This effort to show eight-year-old Laurel the obstacles was Margie's deliberate way of reassuring her. "See, Laurel? There's nothing here that we can't navigate. We'll do it together."

They cantered slowly, then picked up speed as the buzzer signaled them to begin. When Laurel passed through the sensors, the time clock was set in motion. Margie banished all thoughts except the strides to count, the placement of Laurel's legs just before take off, and the time to save with tighter turns. Each lift began with a signal from rider to steed; each landing prompted calculation to position the horse in the proper direction for the next jump.

They jumped the first hurdle, an oxer, and Laurel's rear leg nicked a rail lightly. The fence rattled, but stayed upright. "Settle down, Laurel. We need to clear these hurdles with ease." Margie focused these thoughts toward the mare at the same time she pulled the reins with her left hand and pressed her right leg in the same direction. When Laurel responded quickly, Margie now felt safe to press her faster and tighten the turns.

"Okay, Girl. We need to pay attention to the rails on top of the water hazard." Margie balanced Laurel's front end with the reins so that Laurel would not be spooked by the glare from the water beneath them. She squeezed her calves together to signal Laurel across the oxer. She heard the cheers of the crowd, but blocked out all thoughts except the next fence.

As they approached the Budweiser fence with the six-foot bottles on the sides and the rails in shallow cups, Margie eased Laurel upward, adjusting her body so they could avoid even a breeze to interfere with the lightly balanced obstacle. This fence had fallen for several competitors; and the two athletes, horse and rider, were taking no chances. The successful high jump prompted applause, as Margie turned her mare sharply. "Good girl," Margie thought, "that ought to save us a fraction of a second!"

Next came the oxer whose fences stretched across five feet six inches in width. Laurel and Margie were now responding as one, so that the push of Margie's heels propelled Laurel strongly forward. They galloped quickly toward the treacherous triple. One stride, two, jump. One stride, jump. One stride, two, jump. They sailed over the camouflaged number ten and across the last line of four jumps in rapid succession. The spectators were on their feet. As Margie and Laurel raced toward the last fence, the murmur erupted into a roar. "Careful, Laurel. We don't want to lose the class at the last hurdle." They soared over the final obstacle as the announcer screamed over the noise of the crowd. "The first clean round! Ladies and Gentlemen, there will be no jump-off unless Laura also has a clear round. Margie Goldstein Engle—the first four-time winner is now the first *five*-time AGA Rider of the Year!"

Laura Chapot atop Iko skillfully finished the course, raced across the last obstacle: the fastest of those with four faults.

*   *   *

As Margie and Laurel took their tame victory lap around the arena followed by McLain and then Laura, her father and I eased our way toward the opening where her fans had already assembled. My husband reminisced, "Remember when Margie first asked if she could take lessons?"

"I remember being so worried I told her she could only *walk, trot,* and *canter,* that *jumping* the hurdles was much too dangerous. Who knew her childhood hobby would lead to *this?*" The memories flooded back.

Chapter Two

Enter Smiling

Happiness. Gratitude. Delight. Is it possible that the birth of one small baby could generate so many joyful and fulfilling emotions? Even the little house in West Miami where the Goldsteins lived seemed to glow with the excitement of Margie's arrival.

The year was 1958, and the Goldstein family consisted of her parents, Mona and Irvin, sons, Mark, who was eight and one-half years old, and Eddie, who was almost seven. A little over a year prior, we had lost a baby girl and the empty spots in our hearts loomed large. When Margie was born on March 31 of that year, our joy knew no bounds. Mark and Eddie simply adored their baby sister and wanted to spoil her if only Irv and I would let them.

However, when she began to walk, chancing upon their prized belongings, the results were not always appreciated. "Mark, did you spill my marbles all over the closet?"

"No, Eddie. Did you take my invisible man apart?"

Even closing the door to their room didn't prevent the inquisitive little girl from her explorations. "Mom, she's mixed all the puzzle pieces into one big heap!"

Somehow her mischievous smile, sparkling brown eyes, and appreciation of their every action would win them over once again. "Mom, Margie is going to be one year old today. Who did you invite for her birthday?"

"The family is coming over Sunday for a celebration."

"No *children* for our Margie?" "How could you forget?"

I went about my business until suddenly Mark and Eddie led a group of children to the front door. "Mom, these are Margie's friends. Now we can have a *real* birthday party."

Her brothers had corrected their mother's "error." Quickly, I searched the pantry to find drinks and sweets for this eager-to-celebrate crew.

The Goldstein offspring really enjoyed this pattern of two birthday parties per year (one for the family, one for each child's friends). However, Margie needed a little explanation one year. "Honey, have you put away all your toys? The family will be here tonight to celebrate your birthday."

My daughter looked perplexed. "Celebrate my birthday? I don't understand."

"What don't you understand?"

"We just *had* a birthday party and I was three. Now, the family is coming over for *another* birthday party. Am I four?" Her brothers assured her everything was fine and she was not aging too rapidly!

Margie loved playing with her older brothers, and she longed to join them in their baseball and football games. "Mark, Eddie, I want to play with you too. May I be on your team?"

"Margie, you don't know how. You can't pitch. You can't catch. You're too little. Why don't you play with someone else, someone your own age?"

Perhaps this is why Margie learned persistence at such an early age. The more they told her she wasn't good enough, the more she practiced. Day after day, she would throw a ball into a tire, patiently performing this task over and over until her control over the ball became more and more apparent. Still her big brothers remained unconvinced.

Four-year-old Margie sought the solace of a wonderful imaginary friend. "Okay, if you won't play with me, Teekie will!" Teekie was a little girl mouse who very much wanted to be a boy mouse, and she never ever said "no" when Margie wanted to play ball.

Irv and I watched Mark's and Eddie's reaction with great curiosity, never sure whether they were embarrassed that their younger sister talked to someone they couldn't see or if they appreciated her daily ball practice. One afternoon, Margie's determination paid off. Mark and Eddie prepared for a quick game of backyard baseball, but there were too few boys who could be rounded up at the last minute.

"Margie, now's your chance. Let's see what you can do."

No second invitation was needed. Little and young as she was, she could pitch and catch as well as any of the neghborhood gang. What she lacked in stature and experience, she more than made up for in determination and willingness to extend her efforts toward the required practice. From then on, Mark and Eddie made sure their little sister *always* played on their team. A few years later when she became captain and pitcher of her elementary school's softball team, her brothers expressed little surprise. Of course, hadn't they "trained" her well?

Chapter Three

Home Is Where The Animals Are

The lack of room in our small West Miami house sent us looking for larger quarters. My brother Eddie and his recent bride, Nancy, lived on a beautiful, secluded little lake that we thought would be ideal for our growing family. We built a home large enough for the five of us and one that each of us would appreciate for different reasons.

Irv and I loved the refuge of a quiet country life in the midst of a bustling city. Our front yard faced a narrow stretch of road only four blocks long, so we had little traffic to disturb us. The view from our family room and kitchen at the back of the house overlooked the calm water that included a little beach we had built on its shore. We anticipated entertaining family and friends in this relaxed atmosphere, and I planted small trees in the back yard to shade us from the reflected glare of the setting sun. "Please, grow, grow," I would talk to them as I carefully fertilized, watered, and sprayed.

Our home provided storage space and living space. Even our dachshund, Count Edmark Von Uberheim, found a place to hide when Margie's attention overwhelmed him. Most of the time, he was very

11

patient when she gave him her full attention. She loved to dress him in the family castoffs, and he would stand—still but stylish. Our little clothes designer would pick him up and bring him over to admire. "Mommy, isn't he beautiful?" Count was very happy when he could escape.

Mark and Eddie became friends with Ira and Steve, the two boys who lived next door; and our large front lawn, sans bushes and trees, served as the official ballpark for the neighborhood team. When the summer heat left them limp and drained, the boys simply headed for the back yard where a swim in the lake restored their energy, as well as their enthusiasm.

For the sake of variety, they tried out their fishing prowess. And, of course, if her brothers did it, Margie had to try as well. Since no one wanted to clean the fish, this particular sport did not last long.

The empty living room tantalized and taunted us with its lack of furniture, but it served as a powerful magnet for our children when the weather drove them inside. We soon purchased a table tennis set, filling the empty space and serving as an air-conditioned playground for our children and their expanding group of friends.

Margie regarded Sunrise Lake as her own private nature preserve, and we quickly realized how much our pre-schooler daughter loved animals. Fortunately, the strange creatures that our little boys found so appealing were familiar, not frightening, objects. I was quite used to either Mark or Eddie saying, "Mommy, hold out your hand and close your eyes. I brought you a present." After complying with the request, I would open my eyes to see my reward: a squashed bug, a squiggling worm, or a retreating-into-its-shell snail.

However, Margie brought that fascination to a new high. Jars disappeared only to reappear filled with tadpoles, small fish, or unidentified green slime. Wild birds waited for their nightly breadcrumbs. Even lizards didn't escape the watchful eye of the family zookeeper. She made little leashes for them and happily walked them from one end of the patio to the other.

Our daughter also enjoyed playing with the little girls from next door, Denise and Kelly. They had a multitude of animals, including a mischievous little coatamundi, which is a little creature that looks half monkey, half raccoon. This impish animal would jump to the top shelf and proceed to knock down bottles, jars—anything that would make a loud crashing noise—much to the delight of the audience below. "That's funny," Margie giggled, as her two friends joined in the laughter.

"You girls think that's so funny?" replied Denise and Kelly's mother. "Then you can help me clean up."

One day the girls found four abandoned kittens that could not have been more than one or two days old. Something bad must have happened to their mother, because they were so young and helpless. Margie had little trouble convincing us that she could care for them. And care for them she did. Every few hours, Margie and I fed the kittens with a doll bottle. When they still mewed pitifully, she wiped them carefully with a damp rag much as a mother cat might lick them.

"How did you know to do that?" I asked with some surprise.

"I watched." came the matter-of-fact reply.

The tiny animals thrived, and Margie—as instructed—found homes for all except one small yellow tabby that she was allowed to keep.

Frisky was a most unusual cat. He didn't know he wasn't supposed to like water, so he followed Margie everywhere—even right into the lake when she went swimming. As she splashed happily in the gentle water, he eagerly and furiously cat-paddled right by her side. Nor did he know he wasn't a human. When family members returned to his home, he greeted them by jumping into their arms, placing his paws around their necks, and licking their cheeks.

When Margie turned six and was old enough to go to school, her interest in animals continued. "Honey, what are you doing?" I asked one day.

"I'm working on a science project, Mom. May I use the old lamp?"

When Margie attended South Miami Elementary School where I taught, she often waited in my classroom so we could ride home together. The work of the older children fascinated her, and she longed to be a fourth-grader and do all those "neat things."

I examined what Margie had put together so far and nodded in approval. "Honey, you've built yourself quite an incubator, but where did you get those eggs?"

She explained that she had followed a female duck to her nest and "borrowed" a few of the contents. I smiled. The possibility was far greater that our would-be scientist would hard-boil rather than hatch the eggs.

A few weeks later, an excited voice boomed out, "Mom, Dad, come quickly. The eggs are hatching!"

Yes, there did seem to be a few cracks, but-of course-our doting daughter could have done that when she turned them over each day. We watched for a while and then went about our routine.

The evening stretched from one lengthy minute to another. Our foster "mommy" kept a close watch on her "babies," but by 8:00 o'clock she reluctantly headed for her bed.

The next morning, we woke to unfamiliar sounds coming from the patio. When we went to investigate, we saw our delighted daughter: a happy grin upon her face and three fluffy little yellow ducklings peeping contentedly in her arms.

The next few weeks were very exciting ones for our daughter. Wherever she led, the little ducklings followed. A swim in the lake resulted in first Margie, then one-two-three balls of yellow fluff behind her. When she played football with her friends, her ducklings learned to scamper—fast! And when she simply walked from one place to another, the ducks walked all in a line behind her. Our neighbors smiled when they saw the feathered new residents. After all, it wasn't every lake that could boast of a parade that consisted of one small girl, followed by her own Huey, Dewey, and Louie.

Whether they waddled on two feet or walked on four, it was a definite advantage to be an animal in Margie's world. How much of an advantage, we would one day find out.

Chapter Four

Love and Friendships

School for Margie was a constant source of pleasure—more friends to enjoy and more adventures to seek! Weekend sleepovers, although misnamed, became wonderful events to be shared among her pals. The ping-pong table was folded and moved to another room. The piano was nestled out of the way in one of the living room corners. The girls set up their sleeping bags, pillows, and stuffed animals on the padded carpeted area and settled in for the night.

Many hours would pass before they finally closed their eyes. Pillow fights were a requirement. Then they called for the guitar ballads. Margie's songs touted the hijinks of each girl present, followed by much strumming which gave her time to think about her next chorus. She was no Bonnie Raitt, but her friends thought she was the greatest lyricist they knew. And, of course, each evening had its own variations: scary stories followed by nervous laughter; silly jokes and funny faces accompanied by prolonged shrieks.

And, when horses became part of their world, their activities expanded to include jumping over imaginary hurdles, cantering, and whinnying.

"Is that Margie telling *another* joke?" We would lie in our bed, trying unsuccessfully to fall asleep. "Nancy hasn't stopped giggling since they've gone to bed!" "What on earth are Sherry and Bobbi doing? It sounds as if they're conducting a séance!" The entertainment always ended in the same way with Margie's dad roaring, "Okay, Girls, that's enough! Quiet!" Another successful sleepover!

One weekend, when Margie had slept overnight at her friend Andrea Marks' house, they spent the following day at Gladewinds Farm. Between second and third grades, Andrea had gone to summer camp which included learning horseback riding at Gladewinds Farm. That one day was all it took. Our delighted daughter was completely captivated!

From the moment Margie met the horses, she dreamed and talked of little else. The Kramers, who owned the farm, were confronted with a determined young eight-year-old who would do any job around the barn or in the dog and cat kennels just to be near the horses. For six months, she would come home from Gladewinds and tell her family, "They LET me muck out the barn. They LET me curry the horses."

We looked at one another in amazement. "Margie, what are you talking about? Exactly what do you do out there?"

"Well, the stalls have to be clean. If the horses stand in their own waste, they may get sick. So I muck—shovel out the manure and wet spots—and bring in fresh hay and bedding. And, of course, their coats have to be clean also, so I use a curry comb and brush them with hard and soft brushes until they shine. Oh, Mom, Dad, you should see Holly. When I finish brushing her, she rubs her nose against my shoulder. And Garnet..."

"Yes, Margie, we get the idea. If you're willing to do what you just described, we'll work something out."

After Irv and I discussed it, we struck a bargain with our daughter. "Honey, if you're willing to keep up your good work at home and school—chores, homework, we'll pay for once-a-week lessons."

For me, it was like visiting a new world without a map or guide of any kind. I had never been on a horse or pony, never visited a farm.

As we drove toward Gladewinds Farm, my white-knuckled hands gripped the steering wheel. Margie had trouble keeping still as we headed toward her long-awaited first lesson. I dropped off my bouncing, wide-eyed daughter; and, while she ran to the designated instructional area, I parked quickly and rushed to catch up with her. "Margie, wait. Here's your ticket." I held a small packet of fifteen coupons and handed her the first one.

The fenced-in arena was bare, but the nearby trees rustled with a gentle breeze and shaded the children and ponies from the afternoon sun. Margie was helped onto a small grey pony named Sandpiper and joined three other girls and one young boy, who each sat astride what to me looked like a toy-sized horse.

The instructor, JoAnn Buress, explained the goals for the day, "….and the most important thing you'll learn is how to *post*, how to get in rhythm with the horse's trot. When he steps forward with his outside leg, you'll step out of the saddle and up on your stirrup. As his leg moves back, you'll sit back down. Up and down, feel the rhythm. Now, walk. Now, trot. Cluck—make a clucking sound. Children, squeeze your legs together as I showed you—sounds, signals—you're letting your horse know what you want."

Five little ponies alternately walked or trotted. I couldn't tell whether they were listening to the teacher's voice or following the children's signals; but, as the lesson progressed, I began to relax. The competence of the instructor was obvious, and the behavior of the eager children and gentle ponies reflected their total involvement.

The hour passed quickly. "Mom, Mom, did you see? Did you see?"

"I did. Margie, you were great!"

The instructor joined us. "Are you sure your daughter has never had lessons before? I've never seen anyone pick up posting so quickly."

Margie exploded into the conversation. "I've been watching when you teach the children."

"*You*'re the eager one!"

And that eagerness never left. The next few weeks the children were introduced to cantering. And leads. And diagonals. When she wasn't at a lesson, Margie was on the phone with Andrea or Bobbi or Sherry discussing what they were learning and what they just "luh-uh-ved" about each pony and horse. "And I pressed my left leg into his side, and he picked up the right lead—just like he was supposed to. Oh, it's such fun!"

"Can you ride your horse smoothly when you walk or trot? Are you able to make Sweet Charity pick up the canter right from the walk without trotting?"

The phone lines vibrated with their excitement.

"Margie, I'm so glad you're enjoying your riding. We have some worries though. I heard some of the parents talk about a child at another barn who fell when she was jumping. She's paralyzed from the neck down. We'll let you take lessons and practice on the flat ground. You can walk, trot, or canter, but no jumping. It's just too dangerous."

"But, Mom—"

"No, Honey. We want to keep you in one piece please with all the parts moving correctly."

That simple goal was not to be. "Margie, why are you holding your arm so strangely?"

"It's fine. Really it is."

After several days, Irv and I agreed we could wait no longer.

The doctor's words chilled me. "There's an impacted fracture right where the arm joins the shoulder. If you had waited any longer, growth patterns would have been affected. One arm would be shorter than the other."

He immobilized her arm, tying it to her body. "I'll see you in three weeks. Meanwhile you will not move that arm at all. How did you do this?"

Margie looked at me pleadingly. "It wasn't the horse's fault. I was riding bareback, standing up. It's *my* fault. I was goofing around." This became her pattern. Never could her steed do any wrong. *She* must have been in error.

Her father and I, trying to strive for balance between worry for her physical safety and pride in all the positive character development we noted, spoke to her that evening. "You've got to realize how serious this could be. Margie, you must use common sense around the horses or the lessons stop."

Although she said all the right words, years later we would learn how many chances she took. She and her friends continued to ride bareback, standing, riding two at a time. When we finally heard about those fool-hardy days, Margie responded, "But I was learning to *fall*. I was never afraid to fall, because I knew how to land on my feet."

But, if it wasn't one problem, it was another. From time to time, I'd have a faculty meeting or a parent conference, and our departure for Gladewinds would be considerably delayed. Margie became extremely enterprising in checking my schedule and arranging carpools that fit our needs. "Mom, I met a girl at Gladewinds today. I asked her address and she doesn't live too far from us. She said her mother could drive on Wednesdays."

All I needed to do was to point the car in the right direction. Miss Determination had the names, addresses, and days all worked out. And, when she was older, if there was no car available, Margie found a bus that let her out one mile from the stable. The two-mile walk to Gladewinds and back was undertaken with no complaints.

One Saturday, when I was carpooling my group of ten-year-olds to Gladewinds, I asked, "What do you all *do* for a whole long day?" Four excited voices rang out.

"I should have known better! Let's start in alphabetical order. You first, Andrea."

"Like today—it's Holly's birthday—we have parties for every one of the ponies on their special day. We make a cake out of molasses, oats, and sugar, with carrots for candles. We—horses, ponies, us—wear our party hats and play games while riding. We have horseless horse shows, too, on foot—and we jump and everything."

My antenna went up. "What kind of games are played while you're on the horses and ponies?"

Margie broke in, "Oh, we have relay races. We'll hold the reins with one hand and with the other hand balance an egg on a spoon, passing it on to the next person."

What she didn't tell me is that at various points in the relay, they jumped on and off the ponies with probably more concern for the egg and spoon than for their own safety. Andrea quickly took back her turn, "We vary the relay games. Sometimes we bob for apples, and sometimes we pop balloons."

"Where do you get all these ideas?"

"Well, those are some of the fun riding classes they have at the gymkana shows. But, we work with our ponies and horses, too. Margie is helping me correct some of Sweet Charity's problems."

Diane added, "And mine too. Sometimes Gumon can be a brat and not do what I want. He'll get spooked, take off, and then I'm scared. Margie says he's just testing me, so she'll ride him and correct him."

"You know what I like best?" asked Margie not waiting for a reply. "When we put a dollar or a coin between our legs and the horse's body and see who can ride the longest without the money falling."

I loved listening to Margie and her friends. Watching children grow up so happy, so filled with purpose, so helpful with one another, rejoicing in their own and their friends' accomplishments, I hoped their world could stay like this forever.

When we arrived at the barn, that thought came crashing down as the teacher said to me, "Margie is ready for jumping. You've told me how you feel, but she's so talented. Would you want to hold back children in your class because of parents' unwarranted concerns?"

"Worrying about her physical safety is a whole different matter!"

"Do me a favor. Watch our next group of hunter jumpers. We use crossbars that are high only on one side, low on the other. Where they cross is only one foot high. Gladewinds is one of the most safety-conscious barns in the country. We actually are as concerned for keeping Margie in one piece as you are!"

We—Margie, her dad, and I—spent the whole next week debating this important step. Finally, "Irv, everything I've ever seen out there tells me there couldn't be a better environment for a growing child. They're learning so much more than riding."

He still looked skeptical, so I continued, "I've never seen such compassionate children, such responsible behavior—and I honestly believe all of them—adults, children, animals—understand and read one another's minds. It's just an amazingly happy place."

"Maybe we are being over-protective. Margie, you're such a daredevil. If we agree, will you respect and understand our concerns?"

With Margie's assurances, we reluctantly gave our consent.

As her skill increased, so did her desire for more lessons. "Mom, Dad, Mrs. Kramer told me how good I was getting. I'd be even *better* with more lessons."

"Margie, it cost quite a bit to send Mark to the University of Pennsylvania; and, next year, Eddie will be ready to go to college. We simply can't afford it. Additional lessons are not in our budget."

Our little girl did not let a little obstacle like this deter her. She pleaded her case at home and at the barn. "I'm already doing chores at home and baby sitting in the neighborhood. Isn't there anything else I can do to earn extra rides and lessons?"

Mrs. Kramer came to the rescue. "Okay, Margie," she responded one day. "You're doing a great job grooming and feeding the horses. You sure aren't afraid of getting dirty when you're cleaning out the barn. Let's see how you work with the cats and dogs in the pet kennel."

Mr. and Mrs. Kramer were impressed and let her work in exchange for her additional lessons from Karen Harnden and Penny Fires. Karen and Penny were in their early twenties, full of vim, vigor, and integrity. Margie looked up to them as expert professionals who had gained great experience when they traveled the Grand Prix circuit. Karen had been a contender for the Olympics; and, noting the same ability and willingness in Margie, encouraged her toward a similar goal.

"How's it going, Honey?" we would inquire frequently; and, as a couple of years passed, we realized how wide her knowledge had become.

"Oh, it's just so much fun! Besides my friends asking me to ride their horses, some of the local trainers are asking me also."

"They trust an eleven-year-old?"

"Well my friends tell me they appreciate my working out problems their horses develop. The Kramers say that the horses sell for more money when they prove they can follow directions. The trainers—Bibi Farmer is one—like that I'm capable and *small*, which helps with the ponies. And, of course, I'm already riding and breaking in new ones that were bred at the barn for the beginning students."

"Goodness, you must be riding a great many horses!"

Margie tried to be patient with my complete lack of information about her world. "Not really. Gladewinds has seventy stalls and at least twenty of them are filled with boarders. As the others improve and are easy to handle, someone always buys them. Then we start all over again."

"Does that mean that you're riding *fifty* horses at any given time!"

Margie laughed. "Oh, Mom! I do different things at different times. When they're about two to three years old, I break them to the saddle and bridle. When they reach four to five, we start them on jumps—but only small ones."

Margie loved riding *all* the mounts—the more difficult the horse, the greater the challenge. Mrs. Kramer teased her, "Margie, you would ride a donkey if we had one!"

As they spent additional time togther, the bond between the Kramers and Margie became even stronger. Dorothy Kramer was a patient, gentle lady who thoroughly enjoyed all the children who came to the barn. Mr. Kramer hid his loving nature behind a gruff exterior that frightened some of the young people until they got to know him better. They liked Margie's impish good humor and her proven responsibility; but, even as their "fourth daughter," they sometimes despaired at her mischief.

Mrs. Kramer corrected her gently, "Margie, the sprinklers went on right in the middle of Karen's lessons. How do you think that happened?"

Karen threw up her hands and reminded her young pupil, "Will the Mouseketeer please take the underwear off her head? Her two pony tails sticking out of each leg hole don't look the least bit like mouse ears to me. Besides, enough of the singing already!"

Sometimes she simply answered Margie in resigned tones, "Okay, knock, knock. Who's there? And this is the last joke for today!"

For the most part, they put up with her pranks and jokes, because the work always was done. However, Mrs. Kramer had the last laugh when Margie couldn't find March Lad to "school" (practice or warm up).

"Mrs. Kramer, Mrs. Kramer, I can't find March Lad! You didn't sell him, did you?"

"No. Is he out in the pasture?"

"I've looked there. I've looked in every stall in the barn. I checked the horses the students are riding. Did someone leave the gate open? Could he have wandered into the street? Could someone have taken him!"

Mrs. Kramer couldn't help laughing that her trick had worked on the number-one prankster. "Little Miss, how does it feel to have someone play a joke on *you?* I hid March Lad. If you go over to the dog kennels, you'll find a rather large surprise." Margie *tried* to be a little more careful about her pranks, but opportunities just seemed to present themselves.

Chapter Five

Elementary, My Dear Watson

"Margie, I don't know what I'm going to do with you!" The contrite third-grader squirmed under the stern gaze of her principal. "Look at these report cards for the last three years. What do you see?"

"Well, I do have all A's, Miss Bradley."

"You know very well what I mean. Look at the *left*-hand side—at the *conduct* side. If you weren't such a good student, I wouldn't be so upset with you. What do you see under *self-control?*"

Even without looking, Margie knew that there were checkmarks indicating the need to improve. She squirmed under Miss Bradley's stern stare. "I know. I talk too much."

"And why is that?"

"Well, when I finish my work, I start playing some of the learning games or else I do my homework and pretty soon I forget and start talking. I can't sit still that long. My teacher says I have too much energy for my own good."

"Margie, your mother teaches in this school. How do you think she feels when we have to punish you so much?"

"I know she's embarrassed. She's spoken to me about it. She's told me that people watch me and expect more of a teacher's child, but does everybody have to tell her *every*thing? Last week the custodian told her when he saw me—I wasn't even in *school*—bike riding on a friend's handle bars. Honest, Miss Bradley, I do try!"

"I've watched you, and I believe you, but this constant talking has got to stop. We've taken away your privileges to go to the library at any time of the day and that hasn't helped. You're no longer allowed to play football with the boys and that will stay enforced. We—you and I—are going to make a different kind of pact. Your teacher tells me that you write very well. After you've finished all of your work **without** talking, you can perform your plays for some of the younger children. It's all up to you now. You're going to have to *earn* this privilege. Do you think you can do it?"

"I don't *think* I can do it, I *know* I can! Thank you, Miss Bradley."

"And, one more thing: you can pick whomever you want, as long as your play is about something educational." Her principal nodded dismissal.

As she quietly closed the door, the chastened young student looked up to see the school secretary smiling at her. "What did you do now, Margie?"

"Oh, the usual, Mrs. Peach. I guess I better stop telling so many jokes."

"You have no class here to disturb. What's your latest?"

"What happened to the dinosaurs that bumped into trains?"

"I give up—what?"

"Well, they became T Rex (wrecks)."

"Margie, get back to your class!"

Margie grinned and waved good-bye.

Eventually I heard of this conference and the resulting pact between principal and student. Part of me cringed at the necessity of administrative intervention for a daughter who definitely needed this type of solution. Yet I had been an extremely shy child, feeling a great deal but saying little. That mute youngster, who still lived deep within me, silently cheered my spunky offspring.

During the next few weeks, Margie faithfully finished all her work and quietly went about the task of writing, holding auditions, casting and rehearsing. Some of her actors bore a remarkable resemblance to the "Peanut" characters in the comic pages; but, if Charles Shultz had any objections, the budding thespians never knew about them.

At dinner we listened to how Margie and her traveling troubadours had just concluded one of their performances when she was surprised to hear her name on the intercom with a request that she report to the office.

"Have I done anything wrong? I don't think so," she thought. Then she remembered, "Oh dear, I was telling jokes at lunch yesterday. Did the cafeteria manager report me? Maybe the P. E. teacher told about my doing a jig when she was teaching square dancing. Uh-oh, I'm in trouble."

As she entered the room, she heard her principal's cheerful "Come in, Margie. I want to talk to you."

"How bad could it be? She doesn't sound angry." Then out loud and with a confidence she didn't feel, "Hello, Miss Bradley, you wanted to see me?"

"Margie, I was just watching from the hall through your windows and saw your latest play. It looked like everyone in the cast and in the class was enjoying your efforts. I was surprised to see Jordan playing Charlie Brown. How did he get that part?"

"Well, he *looks* like Charlie Brown, and he was so anxious to be in the play, he's been letting me help him with his reading." Margie was pleased to see a satisfied smile creep across her perceptive principal's face.

"I've been talking to your teacher and she tells me there will be no reminder on your report card about a need for self-control. In fact, she said your work and your conduct have both been excellent. Margie, I knew you could do it if you tried! You ended this school year making both of us feeling proud. Our pact will continue next fall as well."

*   *   *

Because of all the games her brothers enjoyed, Margie grew up loving all sports. She may have looked petite and feminine with her big brown eyes and soft, golden brown hair framing her small features, but the school and neighborhood boys knew better. Often she would be the only girl included in their backyard games.

I once picked her up from an eight-year-old's birthday party. All I could see was a group of young boys playing football. I asked the mother of the birthday boy, "Where's Margie?" Slowly the defensive team untangled themselves from the target of their tackling efforts. Underneath the pile of children was one small girl, a big grin across her dirt-smeared face, a tightly-clutched football still in her hands.

On the ride home I asked her, "Margie, were you the only girl invited to John's birthday party?"

She looked at me in surprise. "Of course. The other girls don't know how to play football."

Now it was my turn to be surprised. Life with Margie would never be dull!

*　　　*　　　*

Fourth grade began routinely. Margie was happy with her new teacher and with her old friends. Then suddenly Mrs. Pollins and I began to exchange students on the basis of their ability in both Reading and Mathematics. Margie was sorry (almost) that she was in the high reading group, because having your very own parent as a teacher was not easy.

As we rode out to our daily after-school trip to Gladewinds, Margie complained, "Do I have to call you 'Mrs. Goldstein'?"

"Margie, when you come to my class, you're one of my students. It's important to me that each child feels I'm being fair, and that I treat each one equally. You'll have to behave the same as everyone else does. By the way, Honey, what a great play you wrote! I'm eager to see how it turns out when you finish rehearsing."

In addition to the plays that the children found so motivating, I enjoyed planning activities for my students that complemented their reading topics. We participated in Hawaiian luaus, Japanese tea parties, and first-hand studies of Florida history which included learning more about the state's Native Americans.

"Mrs. Goldstein, did you see the diorama I made of the chickee and the Miccosukees living in it?"

"I made clay models of the animals you can find in the Everglades! Do you like my alligator?"

"I drew pictures of the Native Americans doing their Corn Dance."

The children grew more eager with every passing day. The scheduled field trip arrived at last. When the bus met us in the front driveway, the students bounced aboard, laden with packed lunches, great expectations, and little-concealed excitement. Hooray! Grade Four would visit a *real* reservation. As the bus headed westward on Tamiami Trail, the familiar landmarks—motel signs, car dealerships, restaurants, and a large track of acreage that would soon become Florida International University—faded from our view. We saw markers, but few street signs. Sawgrass nestled next to the narrow road. Snowy egrets formed white silhouettes against the clear blue sky, while blue herons below stalked for small fish in the shallow water.

The unfamiliar sights created squeals of commotion, as well as screams for attention. One little group was so noisy and so disturbing to the bus driver that I grew weary at admonishing them. "Okay, boys and girls, this is your final warning. If anyone continues to misbehave, I'm sorry, but that person will not get off at the first stop."

Unfortunately, one person was unable to resist clowning around, spreading her "wings," and cawing to her fellow students. When the bus stopped for the first time at the Miccosukee children's school, two people remained aboard: the bus driver and Margie.

At the end of the day, before we had even reached the car, my angry daughter blurted out, "I can't believe you didn't let me see the Indian school!"

"And I can't believe you didn't listen to me! Young lady, do the other children know I mean what I say?"

"Yes."

"Do I ever tell you anything at home that I don't mean?"

"No."

"In fact, you're lucky we're headed out to Gladewinds. Ordinarily when you misbehave, you forfeit a day at the barn. I figure you've missed enough already. Margie, I expect much better from you! You know what's right."

Her silence indicated that she was either thinking it over or that she was afraid I would turn the car around and head for home. Her cooperation for the rest of the school year indicated she learned the hard way that her fourth-grade reading teacher meant exactly what she said—no exceptions.

*   *   *

Our afternoon drives to Gladewinds gave mother and daughter many opportunities to exchange information and to let Margie talk about any concerns she had—large or small. We were both relaxed as we drove the quiet streets of West Kendall Drive; and, as the thought came into her head, it then popped from her lips. Every year I gained more insight into the way her mind worked.

"Mom, I feel sorry for my sixth-grade teacher. I don't think she knows how to smile or enjoy herself. When I was conducting our class meeting today, I told a joke and she just scowled at me."

"Was your joke that bad, Madam President?" I teased.

"Did you hear the one about the snails and their auto racing? One had his automobile painted with a great big "S" on the side. He said he always wanted to race and hear the crowd cheer: Look at that 'ess-car-go'!"

"That's a good one—I'll bet Mrs. Peach will enjoy it when you see her. And, yes, Honey, some people do find life too serious to see any pleasure in it. I'm sure glad you're not one of them!"

"Mom, speaking of pleasure, you haven't forgotten about the end-of-the-year baseball game, have you?"

The annual baseball game between the faculty and the graduating sixth graders always served as a source of great excitement between the contestants. "I know we're going to win, but everyone knows you're my mother and I don't want you to embarrass me." The big grin on her face underscored the teasing note in her voice.

"My, how times have changed! I could have said those same words just a few years ago, but not any more. Honey, since we began taking away your riding priviliges if you misbehave, you've become downright reasonable."

We set aside time for the practice, and the coaching proceeded in earnest. Our front yard once again became a ballpark. Margie provided the pitching and the encouragement. "Mom, keep trying." "That's good. You almost hit the ball." "Look at that. You hit it! Now, run, run!"

At the end-of-the-year event, Margie received many pats on the back as she ran across home plate. As for her mother, well, at least I didn't fall flat on my face.

South Miami Elementary had been a very special place to attend school. On the day of graduation, Margie hugged and joked with Miss Bradley and Mrs. Peach, bid her favorite teachers good-bye, and went to wait in my classroom for her daily ride to the horses. Thank goodness, some things never changed. Or so we thought.

Chapter Six

Meanwhile Back at the Ranch

I turned off Kendall Drive into the gravel road of Gladewinds Farm. The rocks crunched under the weight of the car as I slowly drove toward the schooling arena in the back area. Islands of green pine trees around the periphery of the eighteen to twenty acres swayed in the gentle breeze. The frantic pace of many errands receded from my thoughts as the familiar scenes unfolded.

I smiled as I passed the mare and her yearling in the front pasture. She and her offspring had been the excited center of many car-pool conversations. Dinner time must have been approaching for the occupants of the small-animal kennel. The demanding orders of the dogs created a cacophony of barks, yelps, and howls. The distant whinnying in the background added to the barnyard symphony.

The plain wood barn stood clean and tall behind the main building: a home occupied by Dorothy and Bob Kramer and their three daughters: Robin, Janice, and Terry. To the left was a fenced-in area worn bald by the constant trodding of the ponies and their young riders. Slightly to the right of the barn, and still behind the Kramer home, there was the kennel area including the runs used by the cats, dogs, and other small animals.

After parking the car and walking toward the pick-up area, I overheard Margie's mentor, Karen, reminding one of the boarders about her forgetfulness. "Hey, Your Highness, you left your saddle in the middle of the barn. There are no servants here. You know where to put it."

"Yes, Ma'am," came the snappy reply.

Between house and barn, a group of palm and gumbolimbo trees with benches underneath served as a welcoming oasis where the students rested after completing their lessons. I greeted the sprawled-out, heat-soaked girls from our car-pool and headed for the nearest tree. "Hi, Mrs. Kramer, you've found a nice shady place to escape the summer heat. May I join you?"

"Sure. Your daughter has two more ponies to school after she finishes cooling down Bluey, so you might as well get comfortable."

"Thanks. And speaking of 'thanks,' Margie's dad and I are sure grateful you're letting her earn extra lessons. Having two sons in college doesn't leave much money for extras."

""Don't thank me. Both Karen and Penny tell me how Margie's riding has helped make the horses more responsive to their commands. She seems to get inside their heads somehow or maybe they just know she means business. Whatever it is, she's going to be one of our best riders and trainers soon."

"That's good to hear. We're glad she's channeling her stubborness into something so healthy."

"I don't know about 'stubborn.' My husband and I rather like her *determination*. She's finishing up with Holly. Next comes Garnet. You'll see what I mean."

"Oh, have we heard about Garnet! Margie tell us that not even the professionals can do much with her. Is it true you bet her a can of soda she couldn't stay on Garnet for a whole riding lesson?"

Mrs. Kramer smiled. "You should know if you want Margie to do something, all you have to do is say it's too difficult for her."

"We noticed some extra black and blue spots all over her body; and, when we asked her about them, she tells us Garnet likes to stop unexpectedly at one of the jumps."

"Yes, she sure does. That ornery little creature has perfected the 'art' of stopping short, dropping her shoulder, and promptly dumping the rider. Margie has learned to land on her feet and Garnet is dumping her fewer times. If they keep improving like this, we'll be entering the two of them in one of the local shows on Saturday."

As I watched the horse and rider finishing their session, I couldn't help but see why Mrs. Kramer was so pleased. The fun-loving, joke-telling daughter who would soon be driving home with me was nowhere to be seen. I was looking at a picture of total attention to the task at hand. Again and again they would repeat the jumps. Every successful hurdle would bring an excited "Good girl!" or an affectionate pat on the neck. When Margie rewarded Garnet with a carrot and began the cooling-down walk, I couldn't help smiling at her softly-spoken words. "That's what I expect, you beautiful little girl. We both know you can do it. You're so-o-o good!"

When she returned all the horses to their stalls, a beaming rider joined the car-pool group. Her wet blouse stuck to her skin. Her face was covered with the dust from the schooling ring. One clean streak, where she must have wiped off the perspiration, gleamed from her dirty face. "O. K. Gang, what are we waiting for? We're off to see the wizard—the wonderful wizard of Oz," she sang out happily.

"Not so fast, 'Dorothy'," I said, as the fragrance from my daughter assaulted my nostrils. "Wipe your boots over there on the grass. We don't need to bring back souveniers from Kansas."

Mrs. Kramer was true to her word. When she felt they were ready, Margie and Garnet rode in three consecutive pony hunter and equitation events. As she learned about the world of riding competition, we gained knowledge about the people who inhabited that world.

We both had a lot to learn. Irv rode horses when he was a little boy attending camp. I had *never* even been astride one. Now our daughter's interest was propelling us toward completely new and novel experiences.

The first of the small horse shows arrived on a bright summer day. The air was crisp and bristled with our daughter's excitement. We dropped her off at Gladewinds so that she could help prepare the horses and load the trucks with the skittish animals and all the equipment that went with them. With me as navigator, Irv followed the directions Margie had given us. As we drove toward our goal, we commented on the many horse farms that dotted the landscape in the Kendall area. "I had no idea so many people owned horses. Every home seems to have acres of land as well as barns and stalls," I noted.

When we passed a collection of small stores, Irv added, "Did you see the feed and hay store? That tells you quite a bit about the area."

We located the designated arena, easily sighted by the large number of trailer trucks and horse vans that filled the outer perimeter as well as much of the acreage within the fenced-in farm. We parked on the street and wound our way in and out of the vehicles, owners, horses, and—what seemed to us—an equal number of dogs.

The hubbub of activity encompassed both a joyous we're-at-a-county-fair attitude and a serious, well-performed preparation for the forthcoming event. I found it difficult to identify who was competing. Parent and child were equally busy and identically clad. They wore their jodhpurs and boots with casual elegance and studied indifference.

Someone from this purposeful group must have recognized me—probably from school. "You're Margie's mother?"

I looked at her inquiringly. "Yes."

"If you want to help your daughter," she offered, "you'll see that she dresses *herself* as well as she grooms her horse."

The shock of her advice must have registered on my face, but I gritted my teeth, faked a smile, and managed a surprised, "Thank you."

"What was that about?" Irv inquired.

"I'm not sure if I was just put down by a snob or if I didn't recognize someone just trying to be helpful. From what I've seen and heard, many of these parents are reliving their days of glory. They traveled the circuit when they were children; and, now that their own kids are into show jumping, they take every little detail so-o seriously. I like the fact that Margie and her friends are enjoying themselves, learning responsibility, and getting a chance to just be children!"

"What was this about her outfit?"

"I'm not sure. She's wearing the hunt cap and belt that we got her for her tenth birthday. The ratcatcher, jodhpurs, and boots are hand-me-downs from the Kramer daughters."

"What are ratcatchers?"

"Oh, Irv, you know less than I do. That's the special blouse with the attached collar they wear for the horse shows, and don't ask me how it got that name. I asked, but no one has the slightest idea."

We finally found our way to the bleachers where I introduced Irv to a group of fellow carpoolers. We began to relax and converse with the people around us. "Is this Margie's first show?"

"Well, she rode Andrea's horse, Sweet Charity, when she was nine, but that was a walk-trot class. This will be her first show where she'll jump over the fences. I'm a little nervous about that."

"Don't worry. The fences in these equitation classes are quite low—only a couple of feet tall. The judges will base their decisions on how smoothly the riders change the horses' strides and how well they maintain their position. The judges also look for style and evenness and form."

I tried to relax. Finally, our daughter cantered onto the field. To our untrained eyes, Margie and Garnet looked great as they successfully jumped the nine hurdles. Later we would learn that Margie was an effective, rather than a pretty, rider. She had learned so much on her own that she did not have the finesse that some of the well-guided riders exhibited. When our daughter's fans began to cheer, Irv and I exchanged smiles. "Yeah, Margie." "Go, Margie." If she heard, you could not tell from her focused attention: jaws rigid, brown eyes staring toward each hurdle ahead. That stern look always surprised us.

When everyone had completed their course, the judge announced, "And the first-place winner is—Margie Goldstein." I jumped up, grabbed Irv, and the two of us jumped up and down right along with the children.

We approached the second horse show less tentatively. We knew Margie's group of friends and liked each one of them. There was an air of healthy young animals about the boys and girls. They pursued their activities with vigor, loved the horses they worked with, and enjoyed an easy familiarity among themselves. They respected one another's accomplishments and applauded long and loud when one of their group performed well. One particularly good performance brought Margie's friends to their feet, as they shouted out their appreciation. "Who is *that*?" we overheard.

"One of the *Gladewinds* group," came a condescending explanation.

We ignored the pettiness and concentrated on the activities, the children's pride, and the outfits representing their unique sport. Regulation dress was worn as much for safety as for style. The hunt cap was not just jaunty, but was made of hard plastic to ensure as much protection as possible. Jodhpurs narrowed at the lower leg to prevent wrinkles, and the suede on the inside of the thighs and down the inside knee and calf helped the rider grip the horse. The leather boots allowed the rider a firmer grip around the horse and the attached spurs provided the incentive to move forward. In case a rider fell, the strength of the boots offered further protection if the horse should step on him or her.

One of the children's relatives in our Gladewinds group commented, "I can't help noticing that somehow the horses look better than their riders."

This time I was prepared. "Isn't it great? I think they just love those horses so much they spend extra time grooming them. Margie may not be immaculate, but her horse sure is."

The afternoon competition ended, and once again Margie won a blue ribbon.

By the time we attended the third show, we felt very knowledgeable about what to expect. Even Margie's winning the blue ribbon for the third time seemed to be part of the routine, so we were taken off guard by the remark of one of our group.

"If that were my child, I'd find the most expensive horse available and buy it for her." I don't even remember what I replied, but I had to remind myself that she was saying this in recognition of Margie's skill. Our financial priorities were completely unknown to most of the people in this world of relative wealth.

At the end of the third show, her dad and I expected to see a joyous victor.

"What's the matter, Honey. You *won*, remember?"

"Oh, I'm happy about *that*, but now Garnet will be sold for a better price so that the Kramers can buy more ponies for the students. I'll miss her so much." Her lips quivered as she struggled for control. We gave her a hug of understanding as she tried to deal with this bittersweet moment.

"Margie, if we could buy you a horse we would." Our voices trailed off as she quickly interrupted us.

"I know. I know. I'll see you soon after I finish loading the horses on the trailer."

Chapter Seven

Lessons Learned

We attended aditional horse shows and observed the close communication between horse and rider. "Honey, I know you use your legs to guide the horses. We can't help seeing how muscular your thighs are becoming. How else do you guide them?"

"Mom, to make it real simple—think of the hands to guide the front end and the legs to control the back end."

"Okay, I've got that. Now what do you do specifically with each end?"

"The hands are mostly on the reins which are connected to the bit in the horse's mouth. You pull the reins to tell the horse which direction to go. If you want him to go right, you pull right. If you want him to go left, you pull the reins to the left."

"I can understand that. How do you get him started? You can't turn on the ignition."

Ten-year-old Margie rolled her eyes. "You sure you want to know?"

"I really do. Sorry about that. How do you get him moving?"

"When you squeeze your calves and heels together, you channel him forward. For the less sensitive ones, and only if needed, you use spurs.

Your legs can help him with directions also. At the same time as you're pulling the reins to make him go left, you press your right leg to his side. When you want to turn right, you direct him right with your reins and press him with the left leg."

"Margie, that's a lot more complicated than I realized. Anything else we should watch for?"

"You know when you see me petting the horse after we go over the hurdles? They're like babies. They need reassurance and praise. Also since they can't tell us how they feel, we have to know whether they're afraid or stubborn."

"Isn't that hard to know?"

"That's why I like to ride so many different kinds of horses. Each one is different. Garnet was so ornery that I had to be real firm with her when she was bad and give her lots of treats when she did well. March Lad is so eager to please, that I have to be more gentle with him so he doesn't get discouraged. Really, after a while, you get a horse sense for what they're thinking and can feel what they feel."

"*You* can feel it. I find the same kind of individual differences with my students, but I don't know if I could do that with animals. Anyway, thanks for the lesson. It helps me to understand what we're watching."

The more shows we watched, the more we understood Margie's love and pride in her four-legged friends and the more we learned as well. We now knew that the size of the horse determined the division. The steed was measured from the top of the front hoof to the withers (at the end of the neck, right above the shoulder). The measuring stick was calibrated in "hands" and each hand equalled four inches. Because of Margie's small size, the Kramers and others wanted her to ride in pony divisions. If the horse measured 12.2 hands or under, she rode in a small pony class, 12.2 hands to 13.2 were medium ponies, and 13.2 to 14.2 were considered large ponies.

The Gladewinds group especially loved the small, local shows that took place at some of the farms in the southwestern part of Miami, at the South

Miami Riding Club right next to Baptist Hospital, or at Tropical Park on Bird Road. These informal events, unrated by the American Horse Show Association (AHSA), the overall governing body for all horse shows, provided competition but mostly fun. Often the children would ride the ponies along little-traveled (at *that* time!) Kendall Road, followed by adults in cars, all headed for an exciting week-end show. Once there, they worked out of the car which held vast amounts of equipment.

The gymkana shows gave the riders an opportunity to work as a team, and the Gladewinds group was loud and hearty as they cheered one another through the different relay races. At the end of a show, Margie would bounce in the house, "I won saddle soap. That means I have more money from my allowance to buy some treats for the ponies." Sometimes she won oil for the reins or a special grooming brush. These practical items were regarded as treasures on a par with the golden bars of Fort Knox.

Gradually, as their skill increased, the Gladewinds group entered rated shows with AHSA judges and stewards. These official representatives were there to solve problems, answer questions, and ensure that the rules were followed.

"Mom, Dad, these judges didn't like March Lad. I thought he went really well in the pony hunter class and they didn't even notice."

"Which one was the hunter class?"

"That's the one where they judge strictly on the horse. Remember I told you? In the equitation, they judge the rider's position and effectiveness, but with hunter—it's strictly the pony or horse—how well they move, their jumping style, how smooth they look."

"Did he follow all your signals?"

"He was great! I'd signal him for a walk, a trot, or a canter, and he'd respond immediately. And did you see him go over the crossrail fence? He lifted his legs nice and high and Bobbi said his back was arched perfectly when we made the jump. I'm not sure the judge noticed though. He always seemed to be looking at someone else when he gave the voice commands."

"So it's strictly the judge's opinion who wins?"

"Yeah. I can't wait until I'm big enough for jumpers. You either go over the fence or you don't. That seems more fair to me."

"Well, Margie, *I* can wait! Besides, no one wins all the time."

Margie shook her head from side to side. "I know. I know. But I sure do wish the judge liked March Lad as much as *I* do."

*   *   *

Sometimes the shows began so early, the children slept at the barn so they could begin the many hours of preparation. We stopped by Gladewinds on our way to a horse show. "Margie, didn't you just bathe and groom March Lad yesterday?"

"Sure did. But they have to just *shine* on the day of a show."

Laddie (as he was known around the barn) decided this was a perfect time for a little horse play and turned around to take Margie's sunglasses right off her face. "Not now, Laddie. We've got too much to do."

She was now working on his feet, carefully using the hoof pick to clean out any pebbles or debris that might have been picked up between the horseshoes and the frog (the softer middle part of the hoof). When the sensitive feet were temporarily ready (the hoof care would be repeated at the show after each ride), she curried March Lad with first a curry comb (a soft rubber, circular implement) and then a curry mitt. She showed us the hard brushes, soft brushes, and towels she would use next, rubbing him until his chestnut coat was completely clean and shiny. Laddie took the opportunity to untie her shoes. "Oh, Laddie, you're such a brat." Her tone clearly indicated she thought he was the most clever little animal she had ever encountered.

Bobbi and Andrea were almost finished with their grooming, so we stopped to chat briefly on our way out. "We'll see you at the show, but do you mind telling us what you're doing?"

Andrea continued her efforts and responded as she worked, "Well, we use different brushes for the tails and manes than for the bodies. Right now I'm 'pulling' his mane, so all the hair is the same length. Next I'll braid it and hold the braids in place with rubber bands or yarn. I'll braid his tail into thirty or more braids, and tonight everything has to be taken out."

From somewhere in the barn a sponge came sailing across our way. Without missing a beat, Karen picked it up and announced, "Look what I found. Someone just lost a sponge and has to get a new one." She turned to me and added, "I've just clipped my horse to make sure he's neat and tidy. Horses' hair grows long—even in Miami. We'll keep him warm with a blanket on the few times it's that cold. And we'll be packing soon. Do you want to stay for that?"

"What does that involve?

"All this grooming stuff has to be packed in each horse's tack trunk and hoisted into the truck. Then we'll clean or polish all the riding materials. Everything made of leather has to be cleaned with saddle soap: the saddle, the reins, the bridle (after it's taken apart, cleaned, and put together), the paddock boots, and the lead shank—we use that as a leash for the halter. The clean saddle pads, the newly- shined bits and spurs, the water buckets, extra hay, saddles, and saddle pads—everything has to be packed, stored in the truck, and unpacked at the show. You want to give us a hand?"

At the look on my face, Karen began to laugh. "I'm just kidding. We have a groom to help us load and unload the materials. But all the cleaning and polishing, we do ourselves."

"I can see now why you all allow six to seven hours to get ready! What time did you get started this morning?"

"Four o'clock."

I groaned in response. "Is there always so much preparation and packing for a horse show?"

"Oh, this is nothing. Wait till you see when we have an out-of-town event. Then we have to bring emergency reins, stirrups—anything that might break. We don't know what kind of facilities we'll have, so we bring extra water buckets, screw eyes and snaps to hang up the buckets and the stall gates, additional hay and hay nets, fly traps, shavings and bedding for the horse. We bring everything we have here plus, plus, plus!"

By the time Margie was twelve, the traveling had begun—but only to places in Florida such as Pompano and West Palm Beach. "Oh, it's so exciting. We don't get nervous, because we're having so much fun. But we sure get jittery. Thanks for the new choker pin you bought for my first out-of-town show. I got lots of compliments when I wore it."

*   *   *

One day in the summer of 1970, Margie announced, "Mom, I'll have to be at the farm an hour earlier this Saturday."

"Why is that?"

"You know who George Morris is? I've shown you the articles he writes in my horse magazines. He's so fa-a-mous! Mrs. Kramer is sponsoring a clinic for the Gladewinds students—she's paying for me—and I can't believe he's going to teach us! It's so exciting to have someone who's known and respected all over the world, and he's coming *here*. Would you believe he won the Team Gold Medal in the 1955 Pan Am Games and the Team Silver Medal in the 1960 Olympics? And he's coached top equitation riders like Leslie Burr, Conrad Homfeld and Joe Fargis." The wonder in her voice was palpable.

"Okay, Honey. If you're that excited, we can get up an hour earlier. Does Mrs. Kramer plan many of these clinics?"

"During the next year, she's scheduled Carl Bessett for a couple more sessions. Karen's told us he's one of the country's top show jumping instructors, and we read about him too."

These lessons from the experts spurred twelve-year-old Margie's horse knowledge and pursuit of excellence even further. "You sure are learning a lot. What else is going on?"

"Well, Mrs. Kramer likes me to watch the farrier—that's the black-smith—when he shoes the horses. The horses often need new shoes every three and a half to six weeks."

"That's not very long."

"Sometimes the ponies grow fast and sometimes they just wear them out or lose them. The angles have to be correct or it throws them off balance and it affects the tendons or the shoulder muscles. She says you really must have a good blacksmith or you can ruin a good horse."

"Margie, I'm astounded at what you're learning! Is there more that Mrs. Kramer is teaching you?"

"Yes, she's taking me with her when she buys new horses. She's teaching me what to look for when you buy them."

"Goodness, she *does* have faith in you. What exactly do you look for?"

"You look at their conformation, how they move—some are more athletic than others—and, if we want to use them right away for the school students, I ride them to see how well they follow commands and how good their temperament is."

I felt very knowledgeable the next time we went to a horse show and enjoyed sharing the information with Irv. He immediately asked another question that fortunately was answered by one of the more experienced Gladewinds parents. "If the course is posted just prior to the event, how can the riders remember all that so they can signal their horses?"

"A good memory is one of the skills a competent competitor needs. They have to know the order of the hurdles as well as how to jump over them. In jumper classes, riders have an opportunity right before the event to walk the course and pace off the distances between obstacles."

We were learning.

*　　　　　*　　　　　*

Horse shows gradually became routine for Irv and me; and, unfortunately, so did accidents. We had rushed the boys to the emergency room or to the pediatrician often enough that we could remain relatively calm as they were stitched up or as they had bones reset. We could do no less for our daughter, so we fought the desire to take away her beloved activity.

This worry of ours must have been very much on young Margie's mind. Sherry Cicero told us—many years *after* the event—about her first words when she was thrown from a horse and knocked unconscious. As her eyes began to flutter and she was just reviving, she grabbed her best friend's arm and said, "You didn't let them call my mother, did you?" Concussions, casts on her arm or leg, she would allow nothing to stop her from going to the barn.

"Irv, do you ever get the idea our daughter is manipulating us?"

"Only if we let her. We'll just have to watch carefully to see if she's hurting."

When Margie had competed in horse shows for about two years, we heard more and more about Angelwings. "Angel has the most beautiful eyes. When I talk to her, I know she understands. Will you come to watch me this Sunday? You'll see how cute she is and how well she responds."

Showtime arrived. Irv and I observed from the stands. We were aware of Margie's preparation: the time spent on oiling the reins and bridle, polishing the stirrups, and brushing the horse, as well as braiding his mane and tail.

As she took her turn in the ring, we stared in horror. Time froze. As the pony sharply veered in one direction, Margie—still clutching the slippery reins—slid in the opposite direction. She seemed to float in the air before she fell to the hard earth below. The fear caught in my throat, and I could barely swallow. We rushed in panic to where Margie lay.

Before we could utter a sound, we heard our daughter barely push out the words, "Mom, Dad. That was an emergency dismount."

Later when we were alone, I lamented to my husband, "I don't know whether to laugh or cry."

"I know what you mean. She knows our ambivalence toward her hobby, and her first thought was to reassure *us*. What a girl!"

That night in the quiet of our bedroom, the two of us once again debated whether to allow our daughter to continue riding. Although Margie had always insisted the only time there were accidents were when she herself was acting the dare-devil or taking too great a chance, the worry for her physical well-being was constant.

"She already has had a concussion, a broken shoulder, broken arm, and a twisted ankle. Next time she could experience a worse accident."

"But how many other not-yet-thirteen-year-old-children have her sense of responsibility and willingness to work toward a goal?"

"It's too much. She could have been paralyzed today!"

"You take a chance in everything you do in life. Look how compassionate she is with others and how confident she is already!"

Back and forth. Pro and con. It was a discussion that would be repeated many times over the years.

Eddie, Irvin, Mona and Mark Goldstein with Margie on mother's lap

Margie at 4 years old on pony

Margie, age 14, on Gladewinds March Lad, Champion Large Pony of Florida

Margie and Daydream winning the 1986 Washington Puissance

Make-a-Wish Personnel and Clients (Left:Debbie Stephens and Margie; Right: Autumn Hendershot and Margie with Daydream and Sebastian)

AGA Rider of the Year 1991, Presentation of Cadillac Allante

Margie and Saluut winning 1991 Gold Coast Grand Prix (Saluut holds record for most AGA Grand Prix wins in one year (6) and most overall Grand Prixes in one year (11); also he was AHSA Horse of the Year.)

Margie and Hidden Creek's Alvaretto winning Grand Prix in Wellington (Alvaretto's many wins include 1999 American Invitational; 1997 Grand Prix in Arnheim, the Netherlands; 1999 U.S. Team Silver Medal; 1996 AGA Horse of the Year.)

Margie and Hidden Creek's Christo, second in the Grand Prix in Cincinnati, 1999.
(Christo also won the Grand Prix in Pittsburg.)

Marie and Hidden Creek's Laurel winning Grand Prix in Rome 1997. (Laurel also won AGA Championships and 2000 Grand Prix in South Hampton.)

Marige signing autographs in Attitash, 1997.

Chapter Eight

The Turbulent Teens

Graduating to South Miami Junior High brought about a level of independence that our daughter clearly cherished. No mother right around the corner to be informed of the slightest infraction. No principal who knew her slightest thought—or so it had seemed. And no adult telling her some sports were not ladylike. She especially enjoyed the after-school activites which included playing pool with some of the students her friends avoided. This frequently led to surprising encounters.

"Margie, why do you have such a long face? What's the matter?" When we sat and shared the day's events around the dinner table, we were used to a horse-driven, bubbling dialogue from our youngest family member.

"My bike has been stolen. First I looked for it, then my friends helped me look—it's gone."

"Honey, this is the third bicycle taken. We just can't keep replacing them. I guess you'll have to go back to walking or else perhaps your Gladewinds car pool can pick you up after school." Margie did not look convinced.

The next evening her mood was back to normal. "You certainly are cheery tonight. What caused this welcome change?"

"You're not going to believe this. Remember I told you I play pool with Clarence?"

"Is that the same Clarence—a former student of mine? The one who's so streetwise?'

"Well, you did tell me I should find the good in everybody, right? Well, Clarence knows a lot of the 'hood' kids. When I told him about my bike yesterday, he told me not to worry, that he'd make sure my bike was returned. I thought he was just trying to make me feel better, but this afternoon there it was—right in the bike rack the way I had left it—lock and all."

Her dad and I exchanged glances. "Margie, I'm not happy about someone getting away with stealing, but I sure am relieved about the return of your bike. You certainly have some unusual protectors!"

*   *   *

She also had Mark and Eddie who once again provided us with the experiences that benefitted Margie. We saw the humor—as well as the horror—of the teenage years. We felt that raising children at this time in their lives was a little like navigating through a mine field on horseback. We tried our best to guide our horses through the dangers, but one misstep and we expected an explosion.

Because of his temperment, Mark presented few problems. He had many interests and was an extremely mature child. Even as a young boy, he would question what he didn't understand; and, after receiving the information, would reply, "Okay, that's reasonable." When he reached the teen years, he simply buried himself further into his books, his award-winning projects, and his many hobbies. We worried only slightly about his shyness around girls, noting that this seemed to be typical of his friends as well.

Eddie's playful and impetuous nature often brought on unexpected consequences. Mark, at sixteen, had left home for college, leaving fourteen-year-old Eddie and seven-year-old Margie. We no sooner walked out of the house for an evening when our younger two went to work. "Think you're good enough to play one-on-one football with me, Margie?"

"Eddie, you're seven years older than I am."

"Okay, let's make it even. I'll play on my knees."

The fierce competitors would be so involved in the game that soon Ed's knees began to bleed or invariably something would be broken. One of our favorite wedding gifts, a small, ceramic mother and child, became the usual casualty. I repaired it repeatedly until there was nothing left to mend.

This horseplay of our children often erupted spontaneously. "Eddie, Margie, we're going in the back to get dressed. Don't forget your after-dinner chores."

"Sure."

"No problem."

Within seconds, the wet sponges or the soapy water flew at the intended target. Then one or the other would look for a tactical advantage. Taking the high ground—literally—Margie would climb atop the cupboards and "bomb" Eddie below. They had it timed perfectly. Before we exited our bedroom, the mopping and cleaning up had been completed. As we left the house for the evening, we'd call out, "Great job!" Only when they reached adulthood did we find out how this was accomplished. Their code of silence and loyalty to one another remained a constant throughtout all the years of their childhood.

*   *   *

Both of our boys were bar mitzvahed. The additional car pooling for their Hebrew language education often coincided with Margie's daily after-school trek to Gladewinds. She adjusted and juggled her schedule as needed.

I thought that the timing for this religious celebration couldn't be better. Each son had his moment in the spotlight at thirteen, that horrible first year that supposedly bridged the passage from child to man.

Margie was given the same choice for religious education as her brothers. "You have two choices for Sunday school. You can go willingly or you can go protesting all the way."

We reconsidered though when it came to giving up two afternoons and Saturday morning for bat mitzvah preparation. "I would miss almost three days a week at Gladewinds if you make me go," protested our daughter. "That means the horses won't be exercised those days. I won't be able to be in any shows. It's just not fair!"

"Honey, Dad and I will discuss it and let you know our decision. We would like you to have the same opportunities as the boys."

"But it's not an opportunity for me. It's a punishment."

Irv and I reviewed the pros and cons. We constantly worried about her physical safety, and now she would be missing much of her religious education. Yet, her hobby resulted in reinforcing all the characteristics we valued—discipline, responsibility, caring. Margie's arguments prevailed.

Mark, who had returned for a college break, made the observation, "Boy, she sure gets away with a lot more than I did."

"You're right. You were our first—we practiced on you. By the time we started raising the third child, we held the reins a lot looser. Wait until you have children and have to juggle priorities and fairness."

Mark grinned. "That's reasonable," he said, knowing we would recognize his youthful acknowledgement of agreement.

Mark's visits from college invariably led to a discussion of the war in Vietnam and what would happen when our boys reached draft age. Irv, who had served in the U.S. Army Air force during WW II, felt strongly that the war was just and the boys should proudly serve their country. I felt anger at our government's leaders and that they were sending our nation's sons to premature deaths. Dinner conversation often became heated. Only Margie remained happily unaware.

When she reached her teens, we braced ourselves for an explosion that never detonated.

"Sometimes I'm amazed, Irv. We'll be talking and she'll suddenly tell me she has to go to her room. She says that if we keep on discussing whatever it is we're talking about, we'll be arguing soon. She'll stay by herself until the mood passes, and then she'll come out as if nothing has happened."

"Well, you can't complain about that, Mona."

"I'm not. I just find it absolutely amazing that she can *feel* the change in her mood and leave before we end up with angry words. I talk to the other mothers of teenagers—especially female teenagers—and they do nothing but fight."

"Do you think it's because the horses are such a big incentive? She's so focused and much too happy to want to get into arguments. Or maybe she's just concerned about being grounded."

"Could be. She told me her science class was discussing drug abuse, and her teacher said, 'Margie, you're too high on life with the animals to get involved with stimulants.' Which reminds me, our neighbor down the block has dropped out of the Gladewinds carpool. Her interest in horses wasn't strong enough to keep her from being both boy crazy and drug crazy as well."

"I'd like to hope that our keeping the lines of communication open and her seeing that we practice what we preach has helped her."

"I hope you're right. I've been thinking. She's so close to the older girls. When they tell her the exact same thing we do, it's as if The Word has come down from the mountain. Remember how upset she was when she picked up a wrong lead on one of the green horses she was riding for one of Bibi's pupils? Bibi just looked at her and said, 'No, you did *not* let the owners down. It happens. Stop being so hard on yourself!' If I told her that, she'd tell me I don't understand. When they tell her, she takes it to heart."

"Well, whatever the reason, we should be grateful and try not to worry so much about her staying in one piece." Little did we know how futile those words would be.

*   *   *

"Margie, your dad and I received a wedding invitation from Karen also. That was mighty nice of her."

"That's Karen. I wish she could have met Mark. She would make a *great* sister-in-law."

"Margie, you sure like to hold onto your friends! Is she going to continue out at the barn?"

"Karen is already planning on a family. She won't be traveling as much, but she'll continue giving lessons."

The wedding was lovely. The bronzed and beautiful bride and groom could have stepped from an advertisement. After the church ceremony, everyone convened in the Karen's mother's house and the festivities began. Cameras flashed. Old friends shouted greetings. Laughter floated through the crowd.

The photographer tried to call out his instructions over the excited celebrants. "Karen, it's time to throw your garter. Lift your dress and let your new husband ...."

He didn't get to finish his sentence. Everyone standing near the happy couple were laughing heartily. Karen, who had disappeared for only a few moments earlier, lifted her long dress, raised her leg, and exposed—not a shapely calf and thigh—but well-worn paddock boots!

On the way home, our daughter mused about the proceedings, "Wasn't that great! When I get married, I'll have to remember my boots also!"

Chapter Nine

Juggling 101

Now that Margie attended the upper grades in public school, making time for all her activities required much planning. She knew we placed a great value on her school achievement, and she pursued her education and the extracurricular activies without any reminders from us. She never missed her chores and joys at the barn no matter the weather, the day, or the difficulty with transportation. Somehow, Margie always found the time.

She also found out how to deal with devastating loss.

"Mom, Dad, why did this happen to Mrs. Kramer? It's just not fair!"

"What do you mean, Margie?"

"Janice told me her mother has bone cancer. I tried to talk to Mr. Kramer, but he won't answer me. He looks so sad. I just don't know what to do."

When Mrs. Kramer, truly a "second mother" to Margie, spent her final months bedridden, Margie found it increasingly difficult to face the daily routine. Yet she started every afternoon at the farm with a visit to Mrs. Kramer's bedroom.

"You're going to get better. I want you—I *need* you—to be better."

"Margie, when have we been anything but honest with one another? When I'm gone, promise me you'll help with Terry. My two older girls will be all right, but Terry's so young, only twelve. She looks up to you."

"Of course I will. I—I—," but she couldn't get the words out. She retreated into happier memories. "Remember when you hid March Lad from me? I was so afraid he had gotten loose and we'd lost him."

"Well, you certainly brought that on yourself, Young Lady. With all the jokes you've played on everyone, you can hardly complain about one prank. No more playing with firecrackers though—that's just too dangerous, even if you think you can handle everything."

"Mrs. Kramer, I was *much* younger then."

"Last week?"

All Margie could manage was a shaky smile. "That was last year on the Fourth of July."

"I'm getting very tired now. Before you leave, would you hand me my medicine and a glass of water? And I have something for you. Gladewinds will live *forever*, Margie, because I'm *giving* the name to you. I know you'll never bring anything but honor to it."

Moving mechanically as if in a trance, the distraught young girl brought the requested items, handed over the pills, then held the glass for additional support. When this small task was completed, she stood by the door, hesitated, and struggled with the words she was unable to say a few minutes prior, "Mrs. Kramer, I—I—I love you!"

Margie raced across the field and into the barn. Fortunately, everyone was busy elsewhere, and she could allow the tears to flow down her cheeks without fear of being seen. Her vision blurred, she nearly tripped over a bucket of feed. Angrily she kicked at the offending object and received a sore toe for her effort. She saddled the horse, stroked his mane, and repeated to him over and over, "It's just not fair. It's just not fair." That afternoon, she rode the steed until both were exhausted.

Mrs. Kramer had given the heartbroken young girl so much more than a name. She also gave her love, her trust, and the strength to say good-bye when the time came.

After Mrs. Kramer died, Margie took her daughter Terry under her wing, and they traveled the Florida horse show circuit with the rest of the Gladewinds "family." "My wife wanted you to have this," stammered Mr. Kramer as he handed the sixteen-year-old girl a brand-new saddle. "And I'm giving you my credit card and the keys to the truck and trailer. Don't you take no guff from those kids." He tried to hide his generosity behind his harsh words.

Off they went. Margie matched appropriate level shows for herself and Terry and many of the other younger riders. She sent off for descriptions, prize lists, and entry forms. The smaller shows within the state were not as difficult as the A, B, or C rated AHSA or AGA shows, but that didn't stop the Gladewinds group from dreaming. "Wasn't Katie wonderful at the Tampa show?" "Did you see the way Joe Fargis turned his horse in such a tight area? Do you think any of us will ever be in an AGA show?" After watching a Grand Prix in Palm Beach or Tampa, they even wrote and sang songs that described their heroes' accomplishments. Meanwhile they were not only setting goals for themselves, but forging friendships that would last throughout the years.

In 1974, Margie rode in the junior hunter division, which, at the bigger shows, was divided by the size of the mounts. Small junior hunters were defined as those measuring 14.2 to 16 hands, while those over 16 hands were considered to be large junior hunters. The "really big guys" were yet to come.

*   *   *

The biggest challenge to Margie's carefully-worked-out routine occurred in her senior year of high school. Because her school was so crowded, there were three shifts for every grade. "I'll never have enough time to ride all the horses," she grumbled. "If I had either morning or afternoon, I'd have half a day to ride! With the shift in the middle, there's not enough time in the morning or the afternoon."

"You're right. I've written a letter to the committee that oversees requests for schedule changes. Hopefully, they'll understand."

When that didn't work, I tried again. "Margie, your counselor agrees with us, but says there's nothing we can do. All this has taken time and we're now past the deadline. Any suggestions?"

"Mom, I met one of my friend's aunts. She's a nurse and has to go by Gladewinds if we can get to her house by 5:30 in the morning.

"Margie, do you realize that we'll have to wake up at 5:00—five days a week until the end of the school year!—so we can eat breakfast and do all the things we need to do to get you there on time?"

At five-twenty in the morning with our moods as somber and dark as the early hour, we drove to her benefactor's house. Then I went home to finish dressing while Margie was relayed to the barn. Since it was still so dark, she had to wait until the sun rose before she could ride the horses. Sometimes, when she had many horses to school, she even started as the sun's first dim promise of light peeked across the horizon. She left in time to take a bus home, shower, dress, and then arrive promptly for 11:00 classes at South Miami Senior High School. What a celebration we had when that year ended!

$*$ $*$ $*$

"Margie, how is your schedule working out at Miami Dade Community College?"

"I can't believe how understanding my instructors are! One of my professors saw the Tampa horse show on ESPN and he asked so many questions. He has a daughter who loves horses and he wanted to know mainly about the safety of riding such large animals. In fact, he wanted me to teach her."

"That's great, Honey, but you still are trying to do too much. How are you feeling physically?"

"Fine," came her too-quick reply. "My math prof wants to know how we estimate the number of strides between the jumps. When I explained about our pacing the course on foot, then converting it to number of horse strides, he used the information in some of his mathematical equations."

"Good for him! I like to hear about teachers who relate their instruction to practical concerns. What do you do about tests? How do you get your homework turned in on time?"

"Mom, don't worry. I've worked a schedule out with each of my teachers. Sometimes I take a test before I leave town. Same thing with my homework—that can be done in advance. If they spring any surprises on the class while I'm on the road, I'm handed the same surprise the minute I walk through the door. As I said, they've really been great!"

As she completed her courses with her usual diligence, we tried not to be so concerned about her full days and nights. She was going to college from 7:00 A.M. till noon, then straight to the stable to ride until dark. In order to maintain her 4.0 average, she spent the entire evening on her homework. The tired look in her eyes and the missing bounce from her step kept nagging at our attempted calm. "We just don't like the way you're dragging. I've called the doctor and we have an appointment on Friday. Sorry, Honey, but this is a done-deal." When Margie did *not* argue, we really worried!

The conference with her physician proceeded as we expected. "Young lady, your blood work confirms my diagnosis. You have a severe case of mononucleosis. Since we have no medicine to combat the disease, our only treatment is complete bedrest. In your case, I'd estimate at least six months before you can even try to return to any part of your routine."

For three months, the only time our daughter even tried to lift her head was to acknowledge a friend's visit or to eat—what seemed to us—a pitifully small portion of food.

*   *   *

One morning, Bobbi Badgley came for a visit. I heard the girls talking and felt good that Margie's voice sounded a little stronger. When I came in to see if the good friends needed anything, I could not believe what I saw. There was my patient, fully-dressed in her barn clothes, ready to go. "Margie, what do you think you're doing?"

"Mom, Bobbi is driving me out to the barn. Carole is depending on me to get her ready for an important horse show. I can't disappoint her."

"And what about us? We're worried about you enough without having you disregard doctor's orders! Please, Margie, don't do this to yourself. You could end up staying out even *longer* than six months!"

Neither of us convinced the other. As the two girls started to walk out the door, I turned to Bobbi and managed a feeble, "Would you take her home when you see she's weakening?"

"I wasn't happy about this either, but you know your daughter. She's the most stubborn person I know."

Perhaps her stubborness gave her strength, but she did manage to return gradually to both her studies and her horse routine without the expected relapse. When she received her Associate Degree from Miami Dade Community College, she promptly enrolled in the fall classes at Florida International University.

"Whoa, Honey, are you sure you can handle all this? You're riding and showing full time. Maybe you can delay one or the other, but college and horse training together are just too much. Are you willing to stay this busy?"

"If I don't take a full load, I can do both, but I won't finish in two years."

"Margie, just remember what the doctor said about your health. You've had mononucleousus once, and he said it was caused probably by over-work. You need to cut back."

"I'm trying. Karen, Bibi, and Penny are sharing the work load wth me and that helps. Besides, my psychology classes are fascinating, and the business courses will be invaluable when I eventually set up my own business."

"And what business is that? What if you became a dental hygentist? You'll be able to set your own hours and still have time for this hobby you love so much."

"Yuck, I can't imagine having to work in people's mouths all day."

"Considering what you've raked from the barns, I think that might be an improvement." I ignored the rueful look headed my way and continued. "Margie, you have such a wonderful way with children. How about teaching as a career? You'll have weekends and the summer to ride the horses."

During these years, her father and I worried about a career that would meet her unusual needs and tried to guide Margie's selection. We had no idea that training and showing horses was anything more than a wonderful hobby.

"Can you build a future with where you're headed? We know you enjoy what you're doing, that you're able to make money from both your lessons and showing horses, but you have to be practical. You need a career that will let you be self-supporting."

In an effort to prove exactly what she could do and that she already was directed toward an occupation, Margie announced one day that she already had paid her college tuition.

"Margie, there's no way we'll allow you to pay for your education. If we can do this for your brothers, we certainly can do it for you. Here's a check. Thanks for the offer, but we'll hear no more on the subject!"

*　　　　　　*　　　　　　*

If she couldn't spend her money one way, she spent it another. She lived at home and was able to put money in the bank every week. She drove our hand-me-down automobiles from the time she first started college and found them to be reliable and serviceable. One afternoon she rolled into our circular drive, a beaming smile upon her face, as she summoned us to see her first major purchase. "How do you like my new car?" she asked proudly.

"Margie, it's beautiful! You sure bought yourself a sporty number." We looked at the low-slung two-seater with its sleek plastic molded exterior and added, "Where are you going to put all the equipment you normally carry?"

She opened the door, pushed the driver's seat forward, and—sure enough—she had squeezed in her saddle, reins, bridle, boots, hunt cap, and all the usual paraphernalia she needed. When she opened the trunk, she showed us her portable "office." There were all her files and records which she used for her daily travels. Margie covered many miles and several counties during each day. She had clients from Homestead all the way up to West Palm Beach, and she either taught them or rode their horses at the owners' barns. "Use it well, Honey," we added as we continued to express our admiration.

Margie delighted in that little car for many years, until it came to an unusual end.

"The horse ate WHAT?" the insurance adjuster asked increduously.

"The horse ate about one-third of the top of my car. I had parked it outside the fenced-in pasture under a tree. When I finished all my lessons—which were on the other side of the barn so none of us saw him—I came out and there was my car in shreds."

"Wait till I tell the guys in the main office about this!" Margie laughed when she told us how completely amazed he sounded.

After a short time of driving her patched-up automobile, the next car she purchased was built of metal.

*   *   *

The children whom Margie taught to ride and jump were often from a privileged background. They had few responsibilities for themselves, much less for a large four-legged animal. They found Margie to be a hard taskmaster, but a fair one. She allowed no temper tantrums nor neglect in any way of the horses. Usually she could find something to laugh about with her pupils and turned their times together into joyous occasions. Sometimes the lessons simply stressed both teacher and pupil.

"Mom, Dad, you wouldn't believe the tantrum Tom threw today when I was helping him. His horse didn't respond to his commands, so he stormed off, left the horse in the ring, threw his hat across the field, and just sulked. His mother asked him what the matter was and he started screaming at her."

"What did you say to him, Margie?"

"I let him know that there was no way I would continue teaching him if he couldn't learn to control *himself* and not take out his anger on the horse. I told him that I wouldn't give him lessons if he didn't talk to me and his mother with respect."

"How did his mother react to that?"

"Well, at first she started to make excuses for him; but, when she saw how serious I was, she backed me up."

"Good for you, Honey!"

The next day following this event, Tom called to apologize. A few months later, Margie received a gift and a letter from Tom's mother, "I'm so proud of my son's progress. It's not just that he's riding better—he's so much nicer to be around! Even his teachers at school have commented on his respect and responsibility. Margie, his father and I can't thank you enough!"

Her dad and I treasured the letters from her pupils' parents that told of the impact she had on their children's lives. We were so proud when we went to horse shows and were told about the skills and values Margie taught their sons and daughters. As far as we were concerned, she was also reinforcing good character traits in herself as well.

Listening to my daughter sharing success stories about her pupilsreally gave me such pleasure. Each child is so different, and finding the one approach or combination of approaches is quite a challenge. Whether you're teaching them how to compute or read, as I was doing, or teaching them how to ride a horse, as Margie was, the goals required the same techniques.

We met Carole when she came to Miami, so we understood the difficulties facing Margie, who was only a few years older than her student. Carole was bright, pretty, and personable. She also was not used to listening well to others. Perhaps because her right arm ended at the elbow, her parents tried to compensate for this birth defect by granting their daughter everything she wanted.

Carole wanted Margie as her teacher. She had her as her teacher—even though they had to fly her into Ft. Myers in their private plane. The lessons were often intense.

"Carole, you're not giving the horse a clear signal with the reins. Try pulling a little harder in the direction you want him to go."

"I can't. I can't give enough with the left rein."

"Yes, you can. Turn your body slightly inward on the left side to give more with that rein."

"I can't, I can't," wailed Carole as the tears began to flow.

"Get down from the horse and watch what I'm going to do." Margie showed her rider what she expected. "Okay, now it's your turn. I'll work with your problem, but I don't want you to use it as an excuse not to try."

Each time Margie returned from Ft. Myers, we heard the story of how much progress her pupil had made and how much self-confidence she was developing. When Carole won the title of Florida's Champion Jumper Rider in the Junior Division, two families in Florida—one in Miami, one in Ft. Myers—rejoiced in her accomplishment. Margie had won this title a few years earlier, but the pride in her pupil overshadowed even her own victory.

Chapter Ten

The Road to Success Isn't Always Paved

In addition to teaching the younger children, Margie was also running a "traveling summer camp" for them. When Karen, Penny, or Bibi were responsible for the younger ones that accompanied them on the summer circuit, Margie often had tried their patience.

"The rug is soaked. Enough of the dueling water pistols."

"The hotel manager is complaining that there's shaving cream in the hallways."

"No more pillow fights. There are feathers all over the room."

They never had any trouble identifying Margie as the culprit!

Now, it was a different matter. Margie was in her late teens, assuming more responsibility, and she knew every trick that had ever been tried. Irv and I couldn't help smiling as our daughter explained to us how she had to be a proper role model for "her kids." Under her semi-strict guidance, Margie's students still managed to have fun. Yet, as Karen reminised,

"What a relief to be welcomed by the hotels, and not told to find other accomodations!"

We came home one night to see Margie preparing for one of these trips. She was surrounded with paper: an atlas, the show schedules, and the entry forms. We asked, "Where are you going for this trip?"

"Oh, we'll be in Virginia. I'll call you from the hotel and give you the number. By the end of the summer, we'll be headed further north. As soon as I can, I'll give you the schedule."

Margie was truly learning geography first hand. Additionally, she was learning how to drive a truck, change tires, order feed in advance, reserve the proper accomodations for the traveling troupe in barn or hotel as needed, and handle finances.

"Margie, if you want help from me, you're going to keep complete records!"

"Dad, really you just don't understand. Everybody deals in cash at the horse shows. My clients pay me and I pay for the stalls, the hay, and the entry fees. It's so much easier."

"Easier, but only for the short run! How will you be able to list your expenses when you itemize them for income tax purposes?"

"Income tax? Why do I have to pay income tax?"

"Margie, whether you like it or not, you have a partner—Uncle Sam. Look, Honey, show jumping may be your business, but accounting is mine. What I tell my clients is this: do it the right way! If you do it the way you're supposed to, then you never have to look over your shoulder. Furthermore, where are your receipts? I see charges from your credit company, but no bills that you've saved."

"That's their business. Of course, they're right."

Irv could not believe what he heard, and struggled to contain his frustration. "Margie, people make mistakes. Don't you understand I'm trying to save you money? Hold onto your receipts and give them to me before the monthly statements arrive. I'll check them; and, at the end of the year, we'll use them for legitimate business expenses."

"Dad, if that's the way it has to be, I'll try. But I'm going to have to take much more time—which I just don't have—to do what you want."

As the years passed, Margie always found the paper work to be the least appealing part of her work. To her credit, she does try, but the record keeping remains a constant source of contention between her and her father. As for me, I continued to worry about her physical well-being, noting the constant redness on her inner thighs from riding forty, fifty, or sixty horses a day.

*   *   *

In an effort to save money both for herself and for her students, Margie bought a second-hand truck to transport the horses. Proudly, she painted "Gladewinds Farm" across the truck's panels. She owned no barn, no stalls, no land, as well as no horses of her own, but Margie's career was up and running. Well, almost running.

Even though she constantly upgraded her rig and its various automotive parts, one thing or another was always breaking down. Each new piece of transportation seemed to have its own problems; and, of course, the truck perversely seemed to fall apart when they were far from the place of purchase. Also, there was the difficulty of having Margie drive the truck down winding mountain roads. We worried constantly at the thought of nineteen-year-old, ninety-five-pound Margie trying to control a multi-ton rig as the gravity pulled her hurtling forward.

The horrifying stories were always told many months *after* the fact to avoid any cause for parental concern. "The fuel pump broke when we were driving in Tennessee. I was underneath the truck when a policeman stopped. You should have seen his face when I climbed out!" He had taken one look at the five-foot-one-inch Margie, shaken his head in amazement, and provided the name of the nearest service station. Reassured that she had the situation under control, he departed.

A year later, we were glad to hear that twenty-year-old Margie had acquired a partner for the transportation duties. Fortunately, there had always been friends or parents of her students who shared driving time or formed part of the cooperative truck convoy.

"Who will be helping you drive when you go to the horse shows this week?" we inquired.

"Oh, you've met Steve Engle. Remember—the veterinarian intern?"

"M-m, you've been dating quite a few nice young men. Which one is he?"

"The one I played tennis with—the tall one."

Irv and I exchanged glances. We compared reactions when we were alone. "Considering that Steve is over six feet tall and Margie's so short, he does stand out, Mona."

"Well, I remember him from the tennis date. Lean. Muscular. Do you realize that was the first time she didn't go to the barn on a Sunday or *any-time*? He must be pretty special!"

Another out-of-town horse show arrived, and we received the same answer to our query about her driving partner.

"Steve is going to help you drive this week also? Isn't he extremely busy with his own career as a vet? You did tell us he puts in ten to twelve hours a day at work. How does he find the time?"

"He flies to where we are and then helps me with driving the truck and horse rig. Oh, and did I tell you? He's my financial partner in the transportation business."

Once again we heard about their adventures many years after the fact. With Margie as navigator and Steve as driver of their six-horse gooseneck trailer, they headed east toward Roanoke, West Virginia. They had a full load, and everything was proceeding according to plan.

"Steve, the map shows a new four-lane highway going through the mountains. Perhaps we could save a little time with this route."

"I sure wouldn't mind that. Use the CB radio and see what the truckers in the eighteen-wheelers have to say about road conditions."

"They said they don't know of any problems." For the next fifty miles, as they drove the smooth new highway, Margie conversed and exchanged jokes with the truckers.

Steve looked at the road ahead and said, "Uh-oh, what happened to the highway? All we've got is two narrow lanes, and look! The mountain road is getting steeper. I'm used to Florida and Texas where it's FLAT." At first, he kept the conversation light, but his knuckles tightened on the steering wheel as driving became increasingly difficult.

Every time they descended, the eighteen-wheelers drew dangerously closer. Margie asked anxiously, "What's happening? Why are those trucks right on our tail?"

"They're trying to save their brakes, which I wish we could do. Our truck has automatic transmission. Every time I try to gear down, the clutch slips and jumps into the next gear."

For the next three hours, Steve fought the forces of gravity. As the mountains became steeper, the brake use became greater. Navigator and driver spoke little. Margie watched as Steve gripped the wheel. She noted his shaky legs as he pressed ever harder on the brakes. She listened to the scrambling noises the horses made as they reacted to the sharp turns and the unsteady pace of the ride. She heard Steve swear softly whenever an eighteen wheeler would once again come around a switchback at the same time as they did. Although the temperature was cool, the two of them were drenched in perspiration.

"Margie, I think we can relax soon. I see a four-lane highway up ahead."

Their temporary relief was shattered as a voice on the radio shouted, "Shut her down, Man. You're on fire!"

With complete disbelief, Steve looked into the rear-view mirror. Margie twisted in her seat to confirm the warning. Flames leaped from under the trailer. The terrified horses whinnied their confusion. Steve pulled off the road. Everything seemed to be happening at once. Margie jumped out of the truck, ran to the trailer, and tried to calm the horses. Steve turned off the gas and headed toward the fire. The trucker behind them had pulled up behind Steve and was spraying the blaze with his fire extinguisher.

When the flames died down, they assessed the damage. The trailer and horses were unharmed. What used to be their rear axle was now a glowing red-hot piece of metal. All the constant braking had taken its toll on the bearings and caused the fire. Margie and Steve stood on top of a mountain in the middle of the night with no place to go for help.

The helpful trucker offered a suggestion. "There's a 'kind-of' truck stop about fifteen miles down the road. Would you like me to drop you there?"

The tense travelers considered their options. "We can't leave the horses in the middle of nowhere, Steve." But Margie knew that he was not about to let her go off with some stranger nor would he want her to stay alone.

"Thanks for all your help. We'll both go with you," Steve replied to the trucker.

As promised, a small undistinguished building, giving few hints to its function, presented a welcome sight for the broken-down travelers. They entered into a deserted office and called out, "Is anybody here?" From somewhere in the back, a grease-stained, pot-bellied, red-nosed man, no more than five foot, three inches tall, shuffled out.

After the trucker explained the problem, the mechanic's watery-blue eyes lit up. "Well, this calls for a road trip!" he said as he swung into action. While Margie and Steve concluded their grateful thanks to the trucker, the little man phoned and woke up his nephew.

Nephew's displeasure rang through the phone wires as he ranted and raved loud enough for everyone in the small office to hear. "Hit's bad nuff you woke us, Uncle, when ah finally got me a date with Mary Sue. Now you want me to get myself down there?" Angry words were exchanged, but agreement was finally reached. While waiting for his nephew, the mechanic scurried around grabbing chains and ropes, wrenches and jacks—anything that might be helpful—into the back of his tow truck. The minute he arrived, his uncle threw the keys at him and shouted out instructions to watch the shop.

As they headed toward their abandoned rig, Margie asked, "Why are we taking this road? It doesn't look like the way we came here."

"Well, Young 'Un, the sheriff in these here parts don't like me one bit. Ah reckon he's had it in for me since high school. We wuz both on our school's football team—real rivals, real enemies, right? Ole Charlie thought he had hisself a ticket to college, 'cause he could throw and ketch that lil ball easier than pitchin' a hissy fit. Well, it wuz homecoming—theirs, not ours—and Ole Charlie struttin' and prancin' up and down that field like he owned it. He caught that pig's skin one time too many, and Ah tackled him real good. Reckon you could hear his knee bone crackin' all the way up in the top row. Ole Charlie never went to no college after that. And he sho do hold hisself a grudge. He hassle me, ever' chance he gets—can't go nowhere on the roads, but there he be—hassle, hassle, hassle. So Ah know roads he don't and better we don't see his ugly face."

Margie and Steve looked at his small frame as they listened to his story, but figured worrying about his truthfulness wasn't going to help much at this point. Besides he soon gave them something new to be concerned about. "People round here love to hunt. Can't find no bear, no deer, they'll find sumthin. You say you got horses in that there van? Sure hope they's still there."

Steve and Margie exchanged "I-don't-believe-this!" looks. They glanced at their watches, noted the time of 2:00 A.M., and prayed their way out of this predicament. As they pulled up to the stranded truck and van, they heard the horses nickering a welcome. While they checked out and reassured the horses, Uncle assessed the damage. "Yep, yo're gonna need a new axle. This here one done welded to the wheel."

Steve clenched his fists by his side. "And where in the hell are we supposed to get an axle?"

"In Roanoke for that, Ah reckon. Only take a couple of days."

"We don't have a couple of days! Come on, Man, there must be something we can do. If we suspend this axle, we'll still have three good wheels on the trailer. What if we tied it up in any way possible? The truck's axles are good and it can still drive!"

Uncle scratched his head while he thought this over. "Okay, I'll jack up the axle and take off the tire." Steve swung into action. He wrapped first a chain, then some of the lead shanks from the trailer, around the axle and trailer frame. Uncle lowered the jack a little, then kicked it from under the trailer. The axle stayed suspended in air.

They thanked Uncle profusely, paid him—gladly, and proceeded slowly. At first they drove at a snail's pace, but gradually Steve's confidence returned and they picked up speed. Into the sunrise and out of the mountains, they headed once again for Roanoke.

*   *   *

"Margie, judging from your phone calls, you sure are involved with a lot of horse owners."

She mentioned a few names we recognized. "I'll always save time for them. They gave me a chance when I was first starting out. But, you're right, I am riding quite a few horses right now." Little did we realize exactly how many equaled "quite a few."

After several years of Margie's assuming full and final responsibility for every facet of her horse business, she was very happy to have Spank Deemer join the team. "Mom, Dad, wait till you meet Spank! He's had so much experience with show jumping both as a horse trainer and as a stable manager. And did I tell you about his many years as a football coach? He's really used to handling a wide variety of people."

We felt vast relief when her new manager proved himself capable and caring both with the horses and with their owners. Furthermore, he adapted well to her frenetic schedule with his steady, easy-going assurance. Margie's cheering fans found it comforting to see Spank's trim form rushing to her aid or assistance both before and after her turn in the ring. Easy to identify because of his startling-white hair, the "Silver Fox" became a wonderful partner for over two decades.

*   *   *

Margie's social life required attention also. Although she dated many fine young men, we and her friends were very partial to her transportation partner, who was now a full-time veterinarian. Steve approached his work and his play with the same level of intensity as she did. They not only shared a passion for horses, but each respected the role the other performed with these gentle giants. He lovingly treated his four-legged patients with all the skills at his command and grieved when he could not save them from complications. Our daughter trusted his judgement completely.

When he arrived at our house to pick up Margie for an evening's entertainment, he waited more or less patiently. While she concluded a phone conversation with a client, he talked to us. Later either Irv or I commented, "Margie, Steve is not happy with your being on the phone so much."

"I try to make it short. This is the way I earn a living. I have to be available when the clients are concerned about their horses. Steve should understand. Some of our dates end up with him taking care of a horse with colic." The more time we spent with him, the more we admired his steadiness, his values, and his positive attitude. There was just one problem. Where was this relationship headed?

Her friend Sherry could not hide her concern and expressed the worry all of us felt. "Marge, I don't understand what's happening. You and Steve have been dating for three years now. You both enjoy everything you do together. What's going on?"

From college, Nancy Unger called to say how much she had enjoyed spending the winter break in Miami. "You two are so perfect together. Do you have anything you want to tell me?"

Margie's answer to her friends was always the same. "We're both so busy trying to build our careers. It's awfully hard to plan anything else right now."

They parted as friends. Margie returned his investment in the transportation venture. Steve even visited me when I was recovering from surgery. We spoke about many things *except* for his plans to move to Texas where he would start his large-animal veterinarian practice. I wished him good luck, but felt infinite sadness at his and Margie's decision to part.

Chapter Eleven

Daydream

"Mom, you have a birthday coming up soon. What would you like?"

"You really want to give me something I would appreciate more than anything else I can think of?"

Margie looked at me questioningly. "Ye-e-s?"

"Well, what I really want more than any tangible gift is an hour of your time—one whole hour completely uninterrupted, no calls from friends or clients, our very own—yours-and-mine, time-to-talk hour."

"What did you want to talk about?"

"When we have the hour, I'll tell you."

Over six months would pass before I received my belated birthday present. I wasted not a minute.

"Margie, I've loved having you for a daughter. Right from day one, you have brought so much happiness to your father and me, to your brothers, except for—maybe—the only times we had difficulty with raising you."

She finished the thought for me, "When we were in elementary school together."

"That's right. You sure were a mischievous little girl. That time—and from the time you turned twenty and the years that are following."

A look of shock flashed across her expressive face. "*Now* I really don't understand. I'm on the road eighty percent of the year. I'm not even *here* most of the time."

"I think you've got it! Margie, do you ever plan on settling down? How are you going to meet decent men? Don't you eventually want a husband? Children?"

"Mom, please remember I'm *not* you. You were happy to get married at eighteen, have children early, and then go back to teaching. I don't plan to get married until I'm much older."

"But, Honey, how can you even meet anyone with the life you lead? You're on the road so much, and you don't spend enough time in each place to even begin a relationship."

"Mom, I have plenty of dates, and I've had quite a few proposals."

"But what do you know about them? What kind of backgrounds do they have? That vet you dated up north didn't sound too stable to me—building a shrine made up of your newspaper clippings!"

"Mom, he scared me too! I didn't date him long, only one or two dates and I made sure we stayed in large groups."

"Margie, what happened between you and Steve? The two of you obviously cared for each other deeply, yet—after over three years—you split up."

"I *did* care for Steve and, if I don't ever meet anyone like him, I may never marry. Not everybody feels the same as you."

"Perhaps not. I just want you to be happy. I'd like you to have the warmth and security of family even when you're older and no longer able to work as hard as you do now. Why *are* you working such long hours anyway?"

"Mom, you just don't understand. The professionals are telling me I'm too little for the large horses, that I'd never be able to control them. I *know* I can do it. I'll just have to keep showing them that I can do it. When some of the owners have a horse the other riders don't want to show, they're willing to take a chance on me. One of these days, I'll prove I can be as good as the best of the riders."

We saw Margie's goals through different viewpoints, but I used every second of my hour and thanked her for the gift.

*　　　　*　　　　*

The extensive travels continued. "Hi, Mom. Hi, Dad."

"Where are you calling from, Honey?"

"I'm in Attitash, New Hampshire. You'd love it. The people are so nice, and the arena sits in the middle of the mountains. Everywhere you look you can see the trees with their bright colors and the hills in the background."

"We'll keep it in mind. How's the show going?"

Margie laughed. "Well, there are quite a few older Jewish tourists in this area. Evidently they've read about me in the local paper, because they'll stop to ask where the little Goldstein girl is. The other riders tease me with: Margie, your people are looking for you. Anyway, I won a first, a third, and a fourth in the Grand Prix. This place seems to be lucky for me."

"You did rather well in New York last week also."

"New York was fun for other reasons as well. Did I tell you I saw both Andrea and Bobbi when I was there? In fact, Bobbi was my chaperone."

"How did that happen?"

"When she came to visit me at the hotel, I had a date with a guy named Lou. Since we didn't know each other that well, I told Bobbi she had to come along—I needed her."

"Honey, you may be a daredevil in the ring, but we're sure glad you're cautious about some things. Give Bobbi and Andrea our best the next time you see them."

"I certainly will. Dad, did you receive the checks I mailed you for deposit?"

"Yes, and we see that you're really turning your hobby into a paying proposition. Good for you!"

Except for the time she was on the circuit, Margie lived at home and her bank account was growing. Not only was she earning money from lessons, from commissions when she brokered horse sales, and from fees for riding for many owners, but she received a percentage of the purse when she and the horse won.

Margie rode and rode and rode. Whatever was offered to her, she showed.

"Margie, my horse is acting up. I've already paid the entry fee. Can you ride him for me?"

"Margie, I'd like to move up to a more competitive horse. Can you ride and win on my present horse so we can sell him?"

We'd go to a horse show and never be able to talk to her. After watching a show jumping event, we'd head for the barns. "Where is she?"

"Oh, she's in the junior arena coaching one of her pupils." Or "Well, she's over in the hunter equitation ring with one of the new horses."

She rode and rode and rode. Difficult horses. Horses with potential. Horses that needed coddling. Horses that needed firmness. Thirty, forty, sixty or more horses a day. Sometimes her legs were bloody from all the rubbing and chafing.

Finally, in 1986, two good hunters provided her with national attention. J. Buffet, a large gray horse (16.3 to 17 hands), won many blue ribbons. Sneak Preview, a 15.3 hands chestnut, won championship tricolors at every show she entered that year except one, in which she won reserve champion. The mare became National Champion as a second-year green hunter, and was sold for the highest price paid for a hunter up to that time. Margie attracted the attention of several friends and people connected to horses in various ways.

Dr. Engle called long distance, "Hey Old Friend, I've been treating a horse that you really ought to try out. Think you can squeeze in a trip to Texas?" Margie hesitated. Steve continued. "I think he's a beauty. He's extremely high-spirited and athletic. He moves easily and likes to jump over anything in his path. This may be the horse that will give you a shot at the big time."

"Steve, when you say he's high spirited and will jump over everything, are you comparing him to Puck?"

"No, Puck isn't just spirited, he's crazy! Margie, it's time you stopped riding such wild horses. Remember when you finished the course and he continued galloping—right next to the stands and over the lady in the golf cart."

"That's rather hard to forget. Okay, tell me more about your find."

"He's a large dapple-gray (almost white) Hanovarian gelding, five-years old, and stands 17.1-hands high. When I told the owner, Max Fanninger, about you, he said you were probably too small to be able to control Daydream. Then he saw you riding Puck in Culpepper, Virginia, and I didn't have to sell him any more. He said if you're tough enough to ride *that* horse, you'd have no trouble with his."

For Margie and Daydream, it was love at first sight. Daydream had complete trust in her and would do anything she asked of him. Each time they worked out, Margie stroked and brushed him. "You *are* a beauty! Together we just may make it after all."

Margie pushed Daydream almost as hard as she pushed herself. Gradually, we heard about a win here, a win there, another one at a different horse show. "Mom, Dad, I've enough points to go to the big New York show!"

"Wonderful!"

But it wasn't wonderful. A couple of weeks later, Margie's dispirited voice told us that she was in New York. She had the points to qualify, but someone else was the official team representative.

"Margie, that's so unfair. Are you going to fight it?"

"I could win the battle and lose the war. I'm just going to try harder. Daydream and I are here, and we'll show on our own."

I talked to a friend of Margie's and remarked how stoic she was. The answer came quickly. "She's more vulnerable than she will let you know. I saw her after she got the news, and she went behind a wall where she thought no one could see her. When I heard her crying, I thought maybe it was good to let it out, and I never let her know I saw her."

Irv and I, with great difficulty, said nothing also.

*   *   *

When she called us in the middle of the next fall circuit, we could hear the excitement in her voice. "Margie, slow down. What did you say?"

She enunciated with great precision, "Mom, Dad, I've qualified for all three international competitions. That means I'm now an official representative of the United States Equestrian Team—that's USET for short—and we'll be showing at Madison Square Garden, Washington, D. C. Fairgrounds, and in Toronto, *Canada*! Is there any chance you can come?"

Both of us groaned. "With our work schedules, it's impossible. You don't know it yet, but Mom finally has her own school."

"Yes, it only took me five years as an assistant principal, a year of interning as a principal, three years of interviews and twenty times of making the finals for it to happen. The promotion was worth waiting for, but this first year will be especially busy. Will the shows be televised?" The truth was that it was far easier on our nerves to see the delayed broadcast when we knew that Margie was safe.

The camera faithfully captured the excitement of Margie's Washington Puissance (high jumping) competition. The arena was empty with the exception of two jumps. The announcer explained, "Within each round, the eight horse/rider combinations will use the smaller hurdle to practice, then attempt to clear the high jump. If any portion is knocked down, the pair is eliminated. Another row of styrofoam "bricks" will be added for the next round, and each successful rider will be allowed to continue."

The audience alternately cheered or groaned as they watched the number of riders dwindle. At last only one rider remained. As Margie attempted to tie the world's record for height during a puissance performance, voices rang out, "Go, Margie. Come on, Daydream." The tension mounted. As Daydream pushed upward, every muscle in his body seemed to stretch. "They did it! They did it! Ladies and Gentleman, you've seen a world record tonight."

While the spectators still stood applauding this accomplishment, she was asked if she and Daydream would try for a *new* world record. The crowd fell silent. Margie knew Daydream would follow her lead. She hesitated, yet he had felt strong and was breathing evenly. She nodded. The crowd roared its approval. The obstacles were placed higher until the formidable wall now measured seven foot, eight and three-quarters inches.

Daydream lept upwards, straining every muscle in his body. His back leg barely touched one of the bricks and it fell to the ground. He landed with such force on his front legs that he tripped. The offstride landing sent Margie sailing over his head. I gasped.

I rose from the couch, walked over to Margie, and hugged her as hard as I could. "Thank God, you're here and unharmed. I would *never* be able to watch that in person!"

The film that followed clearly showed an unharmed Daydream desperately trying to avoid stepping on the fallen rider. The camera panned in so close, we saw his foot next to her neck. Spank rushed to check on Margie, helped her to her feet, and the two figures walked out of the arena: one steadily, the other badly shaken. When we made that comment to her, she retorted, "Yeah, Spank does look rather shaken, doen't he?" Margie was able to joke; but, no matter how many times ESPN showed this sequence, we saw little except Daydream's foot next to our daughter's neck.

*　　　　　　*　　　　　　*

"Hi, Mom and Dad. I sure wish you could have been here. Toronto really rolled out the welcome mat; and, even though it's cold and windy outside, we hardly feel it. Our hotel is in the center of town, and all the buildings and stores are interlinked with underground tunnels. You'd love it."

"You're right. We thoroughtly enjoyed Toronto when we were there a few years ago. But, tell us, how are you feeling? How are the classes going?"

"I can't believe how the Canadians love their showjumpers! Ian Millar, remember? I told you he won the World Cup, not once—but twice! Anyway, he's a national hero. They call him Captain Canada, and the news media follow him wherever he goes. The royal family sends a personal representative from Great Britain for our international shows, and the stands are filled for all the events. There are twenty thousand eager fans for almost every class. For the evening classes, everyone wears long gowns and tuxedos."

"Sounds mighty exciting. What about the high jumping class—how did you and Daydream do?"

"Oh, you mean the puissance?" Margie described her experience.

On the scheduled night, she and Daydream waited in the designated area, a small schooling arena where the riders could warm up the horses over *small* jumps. The puissance competition is so difficult for the horse and its slender legs that a concerned rider will never add to that strain with larger fences. Because success in this class is based—not just on talent alone—but on complete trust of each of the partners for one another, only a small number of rider-horse combinations competed.

As Margie and Daydream soared over the practice fence and cantered toward the high jump, the crowd fell silent. Six feet, five inches jumped and cleared smoothly. Success. The wall was raised. And raised again. Soon additional wooden "bricks" brought the wall to seven feet. Margie felt Daydream's heart beat faster. Once again, they cleared the high jump. Margie listened to the sound of Daydream's loud breathing. "Okay, Good

Buddy, you're doing fine. Let's go for it." The murmur in the crowd buzzed through the stadium as they watched the height of the fence soar upward.

At seven feet, four inches, it now looked like the side of a building. All Margie heard was the sound of her own heart pumping blood and adrenaline through every inch of her body. Would Daydream follow her guidance? As Margie and Daydream cleared the wall, the murmur of the crowd thundered to a pulsating roar. The "thrill of victory" surged through her being as she hugged her scopey steed.

Later that evening, Margie—still in her riding clothes—was introduced to an elegantly-clad duchess from Great Britain. Her silver-gray hair was adorned with a glittering diamond tiara. The satin sash across her impressive ball gown displayed a variety of jeweled medals. Her assured and regal voice rang out, "I say, are you the little girl who won the puissance earlier?" Margie acknowledged the recognition.

The duchess leaned over, tapped Margie's riding breeches with her cane, and asked with great dignity, "Young Lady, do you have *balls* down there?"

Overhearing the conversation, Frank Chapot, who had been in six consecutive Olympic Games and who was now serving as the team's chef d' equipe, inquired, "Did I hear what I thought I heard? What did you answer?"

Margie shook her head and blinked her eyes. "For the first time in my life, I was speechless!" Show jumping did have its surprises.

Among the happy surprises and delights, the Puissance Trophy in Washington was retired in honor of Daydream and Margie's winning performances three years in a row. Also, this Terrific Twosome were the only horse and rider combination to win all three puissance classes in one year during the Indoor Circuit International.

Their outstanding wins in specifically identified qualifying Grand Prix events earned them a spot for their first World Cup competition in Gothenburg, Sweden in 1988.

"Isn't it exciting? We have a wonderful team. USET will pay for all our expenses—bringing the horses over by plane, the hotel where we're staying. I can't believe I'm going to Europe!"

Margie's elation was short-lived. Her weekly phone call home began in a low, dispirited voice, "Mom, Dad, one of the riders has offered to buy Daydream from Max at a price he doesn't feel he can refuse. It looks as if I won't be going to Sweden after all."

"On, no. Why can't Max sell him *after* the World Cup?"

"The talk is that if I have no horse to ride, the next ranked rider will have an opportunity to move up and become our U.S. representative. I can't believe this is happening."

"Mighty Mite, even you can't jump without a horse! This is much too important to your career. What if we're able to raise the money?"

Within the next month, Margie's dad, using his knowledge as a certified public accountant plus the services of a lawyer, had a proposal ready. The legal document looked impressive. It included pictures and outlined the financial requirements for owning shares in *Daydream, Inc.* Margie, her dad, and I approached any and all likely candidates and compared results. "Any luck yet?'

"No, not a nibble. Unfortunately, a recent law has minimized the tax advantages in such a venture, and people aren't anxious to gamble. They want their money to work for them."

As the weeks went by and no shares were sold, we finally admitted defeat.

An SOS went out to all the family, telling about the projected sale of Daydream and how Margie would *not* be able to go to the World Cup without him. "How would you like to own a portion of a horse? You can have the end that eats." Uncle Wally and Aunt Dee Berman, Uncle Eddie and Aunt Nancy Pastroff, her father and I, as well as Margie herself, pooled our resources and reached the owner's asking price. Each of us jokingly identified the portion of Daydream we now claimed financially. For the first time in her life, Margie owned a horse—even if it was only *part* ownership!

Soon Margie's "stable" expanded even further. One evening after a busy Houston horse show, Margie was catching up with her laundry. As luck would have it, right near the laundermat was a pet store. As Margie browsed through the aisles, one particularly appealing little dachshund caught her eye. Every time she came back from checking her clothes, Margie told everyone, "He just seemed to talk to me." From that moment on, "Oscar Meyer" and Margie became inseparable. He followed her wherever she went, traveled to most of the horse shows, and—somehow or other—managed to avoid being crushed as he played among his horse friends.

Oscar appealed to many of Margie's interviewers who found it easy to find her stables when they spotted his familiar low-slung form darting in and out of the backstage showgrounds.

"Margie, you're developing quite a reputation as a 'catch rider.' Why is this?" asked one reporter.

"I think I've always been a catch rider. I'll ride any horse at any time, even if someone offers that horse at the last minute. Naturally, I prefer to know a horse before I go into the ring, but I haven't always had that luxury."

Luxury? Margie often rode as many as sixty-five rounds in one day! The years of riding the most difficult horses "any time, any place" were now paying off. Margie had developed a "horse sense" and the horses responded with their best effort. If clients owned large, slightly rebellious horses, somehow they thought of her and her ability to capitalize on the horses' strengths. The horses trusted her, as she did them. Margie coaxed the best from them all, employing what some announcers called the "Goldstein Growl." Her verbal encouragement often steered many a reluctant mare or stallion to make that extra effort.

Chapter Twelve

The Big Push

Along with recognition came support from fans. We enjoyed reading their letters as much as our daughter did. We were not surprised when she heard from many children, but we reacted with astonishment that so many adults wrote to her. Young adults often spoke glowingly about how gutsy she was or thanked her for words of advice she gave when they saw her at shows or wrote to her. Older individuals confided personal experiences, even to tell her when they had lost a spouse or other loved one.

"Margie, this letter sounds as if you've written to her before."

"Oh, I always answer the mail I receive."

"When on earth do you find the time?"

"I have to spend so much time in airports or airplanes. That's when I take care of my correspondence and—*other paper work*," she answered, emphasizing the last three words for the benefit of her father.

"And well you should," came the unruffled reply.

Although fans and owners accepted her well, her dad and I wondered about her reception from other riders. This question was answered for us in Tampa. After the evening events were over, we looked around the fairground for our daughter. We noticed a rather large crowd still in their riding outfits. As the laughter erupted from the group, we noticed a tiny figure in the center busy telling one joke after another. Who else? It was Margie—still the class clown who always left them laughing.

Behind the laughter, there was mutual respect. Show jumping is a sport in which the more the rider observes and listens to the top horsemen and trainers, the more he or she learns. Even to this day, Margie still critiques the tapes of her performance and those of the other top equestrians.

"Great job, Margie! Think we'll be riding togther in the World Cup?" encouraged Olympian and Pan Am champion, Michael Matz, one of the riders Margie watched every time he mounted a horse.

Rodney Jenkins, the charming red-haired Southerner, who was one of the best riders of the century with over seventy grand prix wins to his credit, told Spank, "That's the toughest little gal I've ever seen. She could probably go b'ar (bear) hunting with a switch."

"I liked your interview, Little One," noted Mark Leone, one of three brothers who had brought an added interest to equestrian sports.

"Well done, Old Friend." Margie turned around at the sound of a familiar voice. The surprised look on her face brought a bemused smile to his.

"Steve, what are you doing here in Palm Beach?"

"It's a long, sad story, and I really don't want to talk about it. For your information, I no longer live in Texas. I've moved back to North Miami. I'm working at the track, taking care of their horses, and doing extra work at the horse shows."

Margie took a long look at his gaunt frame and unhappy eyes and decided no further questions were necessary. "Steve, am I glad to see you! Come take a look at Daydream. He's everything you said he would be." Both of them continued their conversation as if there had not been a four-year interruption.

      *   *   *

"Where are you calling from, Marge?"

"Your mail is piling up. Where will you be next during the next two weeks?'

Keeping up with Margie's travels was becoming increasingly difficult. One of the horse magazines found it so interesting that they printed a map of the United States and traced the route that Margie had covered in one year. This whirlwind coverage, as well as the many horses she was showing, led to several unusual records: "Only Rider to Win Grand Prixes in Two Cities in a Twenty-Four Hour Period," "Only Rider to Place First, Second, Third in One Grand Prix," "Only Rider to Place Four Horses in One Grand Prix," and "Only Rider to Place First Through Fifth in a Single Grand Prix," plus "Most Wins (Thirteen) for a Rider in One Season."

With so many wins, Margie began to overtake Jeffrey Welles for the coveted AGA Rider of the Year 1989. This recognition is based on the number of points earned at AGA weekly competitions. For example, the first-placed rider, who receives 30% of the announced winnings, might win a purse of $30,000, the second-place rider, who receives 22%, would win $22,000, and each rider down the line would earn less until the last placement (which could be ten through twelve, depending on the total purse of the Grand Prix class) might win $1000. The money goes to the horse's owner, but the rider earns a percent of the winnings plus receiving one computer point for every thousand dollars won and one point for every clear round.

Jeff teased Margie as her points accumulated, "So you're going to make it hard for me, huh? I guess I'll just have to win big in the next class."

Her retort came in the same easy comraderie, "You didn't think I'd let you off easy, Jeff. I'm going to make you really work for every point you earn."

The two riders were so close that the final competition of the year would decide who would be that year's champion. Neither rider had to *win* the final AGA Grand Prix in Tampa. One simply had to have a better score than the other.

We sat in the stands surrounded by friends and fans of Margie's who drove or flew from Miami just to be there for her biggest challenge to date.

Margie rode before Jeff, because he was slightly ahead of her going into the competition. She gave Daydream a final hug, and the two athletes rode into the arena. Daydream bolted slightly at the noise that rose from the spectators. Margie quickly brought him under control and began the course. They seemed to glide across the jumps. Suddenly one of the planks fell to the ground, along with Margie's hopes and dreams.

Jeff followed. If he rode a perfect round, the crown was his. As he circled the field, he approached each hurdle with caution. He was wise to be so careful. The friends and family of each rider gasped. A rail was down. Who was the winner? With both of them tied in this round, the one with the fastest time would receive the higher score in the rankings. The judges checked the time and checked again. By only seconds, Margie had become the 1989 AGA Rider of the Year. The Cadillac sponsor handed her the keys to her new Cadillac Allante, and Margie took her "victory gallop" around the field, waving happily to one and all.

At the gala celebration that evening, we met many of the owners for whom Margie rode. Max Fanninger, who spent his youth in Austria but was now an American citizen, charmed us with his proper European manners and accent, as well as his knowledge of horses.

Jacob Friedus had been in New York real estate, but was now retired. In his younger days, he rode and competed in horse shows and his knowledge was extensive. We recognized his name from the many phone calls he made to our daughter. In his day, riding was not so sophisticated, so he thought the care Margie provided was pampering. I had watched her face as he argued with her, "Leg wraps? Blankets? Are you trying to spoil my horses?" But they were his babies; and, even though he couldn't travel to many shows, he knew everything that happened as a result of his daily calls to Margie and the show's personnel.

Winning her first national championship opened up still more opportunities. Several clients, who trusted her judgement totally, sent her to Europe to purchase horses that she considered had promise.

When she returned we asked, "How was your first trip to Europe, Honey?" She gave us the names of several horses and the people she had purchased them for. "Great! Hopefully, they'll fulfill your expectations. What sights did you see?"

"Well, we had such a rushed trip that I saw only horse barns. Beautiful barns, especially the ones in Germany. I couldn't get over how clean they were and how elaborately they were built! They served us lunch in one of the barns and it was like dining in an elegant hotel."

"Were you able to see anything else?"

"No. Patti Harnois—my friend from Massachusetts, we help each other—Max, and I drove from one country to another, one barn to another. I had to show horses the next day after we flew home."

"Oh, Margie, you're the only one I know who goes to Europe and sees only barns—what a shame!"

When other sports-minded owners offered her a chance at horses that already had victories in lesser classes, she welcomed the opportunity. Margie was all set to ride one stallion that showed enormous potential. Two days prior to the scheduled Sunday event, she received a call.

The voice on the phone was low and emotionless, but the words chilled her, "Margie, if you ride this horse, you'll have an accident."

She was sure she had heard incorrectly. "What did you say?" The caller repeated his message in the same ominous tone.

"Who is this? Why are you threatening me?"

"You don't have to know who this is. The horse's owner owes one of the van companies money and we won't let any of his horses show until he pays us."

"I'll call the police. Your problem is not with me. I've never even shown any of his horses."

"You can call anyone you want. If you ride his horse, you'll be hurt or we'll hurt one of the horses. If it doesn't happen Sunday, it'll happen another day. You'll always have to expect us."

We watched the concern in our daughter's face; and, even though we could only hear her end of the conversation, we knew something was not right. "What's going on? That did not sound good."

She replied in an incredulous voice. "I can't believe they're threatening me. I've never been on the horse. I've never had dealings with the horse owner. Why are they after me because the owner owes money to a moving van company?"

The menacing phone call had accomplished what the unknown terrorist had desired. I looked at Irv's worried face and wondered if it reflected the raw concern I felt in every fiber of my body. "Margie, you don't intend to ride the horse, do you?"

"I don't see how I possibly can under these circumstances."

When she talked to the owner, explaining her reasons for turning down his horse, he agreed that he would pay his long-owed debts. "You'll start with a clean slate," he said. "I've watched you ride and I really want you to show my horse. What would it take to make that happen?"

Margie responded. "I don't ever want to be in a position like that again. Several of the riders told me that they've shown your horses and never been paid. The same thing with the blacksmiths. The stall owners say you're slow in paying them too. I'll only ride your horse if you let me handle the finances. Your horse is wonderful. Once you're paid up to date, I'll pay the future expenses—entry fees, stall rentals, blacksmiths, and feed— and you'll repay me from the horses' winnings."

It took a full year before her gamble paid off. All of his bills were paid on time by Margie. When his horses won, she took out her percentage of the winnings, paid off any bills that were due, and sent him the remainder.

When he complained about having to wait for his share, Margie's retorted, "Tell me what bank will give you an interest-free loan for a year!" He was silenced, but only temporarily. Margie sold one of his horses a few weeks later, and he was back on the attack. "That was an easy sale. You can have exactly half of your commission."

"I don't believe you understand. I'm following the guidelines—no more, no less. You owe me a full commission."

"That depends of how you look at it. Take half. It's more than you would have had before the horse was sold."

"As I said, I don't think you realize what is involved. I've trained the horse and won ribbons with him. This increases his value. I've had to schedule viewings and fly back to show him. All of this takes time."

"You don't have to tell me. I've had a lot of experience. You're just getting started. You need to take anything you can get. Take half."

On and on, they went. After two hours, Margie said, "I can't take this constant haggling. You want your horses back? I'll ship them back—C.O.D."

"Fine. You want to lose your commission, that's okay with me."

The next day, he was back on the phone. "Okay, you don't have to send the horses here. Take your full commission."

"You mean you kept me on the phone two hours and you were ready to concede the whole time!"

"Well, you can't blame me for trying."

The next time we saw our daughter, she brought us up to date on her dealings with a man so wealthy, but so incapable of paying his debts. I answered, "What a penny-pincher! You must be totally frustrated."

"I sure wish I could tell him where to go, but did you know that even the government can't seem to do that? I've been reading in the paper that he already has been in jail for non-payment of taxes. So, at least I've been paid, even if I have to fight for every dollar due."

"You'll be doing more than reading the paper soon. It seems Uncle Sam is determined to get what is due them also. Dad was contacted by the IRS and they're increasing their pursuit of your client. The agent said they've already invested twenty years and they want closure. They're requiring a copy of every single financial dealing you've ever had with him.

Fortunately, with a little prodding from your father, all your records are complete!"

A stunned taxpayer replied, "Dad, it may have taken me a while, but I'm so glad you forced your advice upon me. I hate the extra time I have to spend keeping good records, but I'm sure relieved I don't have to look over *my* shoulder!"

         *   *   *

"Margie, you sound terrible. What's happened?"

"Mom, Dad, please don't worry. I've been to the best sports doctors here in Tampa. My left leg is in a plaster cast."

"Oh, no! No! Why? What happened? What did the doctors say?"

She named a horse we knew that weighed over two-thousand pounds. "He really was trying; but, as we turned a corner, he slipped, landed on his side with my foot—under his full weight—caught between the saddle and metal stirrup. The x-rays show that all the small bones in that foot and ankle are crushed."

"Margie, we want to know everything. What is the prognosis?"

She paused, but knew that we would find out one way or another. "They tell me that I'll never walk normally again and—because of the nerve damage—they question whether I'll ever ride again."

Margie's wins had qualified her for a long-held dream, the American International, which was a week away. Laden down with a plaster cast, she attempted to compete. As she sat on the horse, spasms of pain contorted through her body. The absolute agony prevented her from continuing. She was devastated. In ten weeks, she tried again using a specially constructed boot on the painful, raw-nerved foot.

"Honey, how are you doing? We're quite concerned about your using only one stirrup while you're showing. Doesn't that throw you off balance?"

"Well, it sure doesn't help. But, would you believe I placed in the top three in my first two grand prix since returning? One of the horses I'm now riding is called Saluut II. Remember you met his owner, Jacob Friedus, in Tampa? He looks a lot like Daydream—also dapple gray. He's a Dutch-bred stallion and stands 16.2 hands tall. More importantly, he's a real champion. He has so much heart and he's so-o-o careful. Anything I ask of him he does! Saluut is the finest horse I ever rode!"

In spite of the pain and the inability to feel the horse's reactions or perhaps *because* of this, Margie was more determined than ever. She had her boot painted black, trying to hide her infirmity; but, at this point, the fans knew all about her condition. She could not walk around the fairground and used the golf carts to get from one ring to another. But put her on a horse and that was another story! Even with so much time lost because of her injury, she managed to end the 1990 year in the top ten of the final standings.

Nineteen ninety-one bristled with activity. In his book, *National to National, A Year on the Show Jumping Circuit,* sportswriter David W. Hollis writes about the events of that year. It began with a burst of patriotism in support of the U.S. fighters in the Persian Gulf. Course designer Steve Stephens featured red, white and blue hurdles with large yellow ribbons tied on the jump standards. During the year, scandal broke out when one of the show jumping horses was viciously attacked. Also, one of the major riders sued the United States Equestrian Team. And, of course, the intensity and expertise of the riders as they traveled and competed throughout the year kept the reader captivated from one page to the next.

"Irv, I love this book. Not only is it extremely well written, but Margie has a chapter of her own—Little Lady on a Big Roll." I read and reread the accounts of our daughter's successful pursuits and creative air travel. I laughed as the author described Puck as a "moose in horse's clothing" and agreed with his description of Margie as starting out minus the money to buy fancy, made horses or the connections to get them.

Still noticeably limping in that year following her injury, Margie rode to win six Grandprix events, including the Attitash Equine Festival for the second year in a row. Also, she placed four horses in a single Grand Prix competition. She earned her way through qualifying competitions to become a member of several United States Equestrian Teams (USET), won her second Rider of the Year Award, and was an odds-on favorite to compete for the United States in the Olympics.

The 1989 Rider of the Year Award had been close. The 1991 competition with Saluut and Daydream both available resulted in a hard-fought, but easy win for Rider of the Year. With this second national award, *Sports Illustrated* featured Margie and her mounts in their only recognition to date of a show-jumping athlete.

"Margie, that was absolutely a terrific article about you in *Sports Illustrated!* They wrote about you and Saluut quite positively."

"They sure did. When people see Saluut's name on the license plate of my car, they honk at me and give me the 'Okay' sign with their fingers."

"Well, that could be because Wellington is horse country and the Palm Beach people recognize his name. How's your new home? Are you meeting many of your neighbors?"

"Oh, it's great place to live, and I love this area. I'm so glad to own a house up here rather than renting a place for three months of the circuit year."

With the second Rider of the Year Award came her second Cadillac. Her father and I congratulated her. "Margie, that's wonderful! Will they let you take the money instead of another car?"

"I didn't ask them. I've arranged to trade in my first Cadillac for one of your choice. I didn't think you wanted a convertible, but they have many for you to select from."

"That's extremely generous of you, but we can't accept it."

"Why? Would you deny me that pleasure?"

When we saw how delighted our daughter was, we tried to accept her gracious gift in the same spirit.

*   *   *

We rejoiced in her career accomplishments, but there always seemed to be a new worry around. "You're going to Europe *alone*?" or "What's going on with Steve? Are you dating any one else?"

Sherry, Bobbi, and Nancy were all married at this point and they too pressured Margie. "How many years are you and Steve going to date?" "Your body clock is ticking, Old Girl." "So, what about the guy from New York who keeps calling you? And the one in Miami that wants to give you an engagement ring?"

We listened to our daughter's lament about her closest friends badgering her, but the reality was Irv and I were very happy to have them voice our concerns.

Although she was still limping, she had recovered from her most serious injury to date. Winning two Rider of the Year Awards encouraged Margie toward pursuing her childhood dream of representing her country in the Olympic Games.

As soon as Irv and I heard Margie's voice, we anticipated bad news. She sounded low and dispirited on the phone. "Mom, Dad, you won't believe what happened. I'm in New York checking on Saluut. There's been a breeding accident, and Saluut's hind leg has been injured. We don't know if he can ever show again."

I heard a loud intake of air and realized it had come from me. "Oh, Margie, that's horrible. You must be terribly disappointed!"

Irv's voice sounded as barely-in-control as mine. "Is there any chance that you can enter the trials with Daydream?"

"I'll try. Daydream is a great horse, but not quite as consistent as Saluut."

"You're right. Saluut has broken so many records. He's amazing!"

She and Daydream entered the Olympic trials, but were unable to make the top four spots. Her disappointment in not representing her country in Barcelona was shared by family and friends. Irv and I, as well as Margie's aunt and uncle, cancelled our reservations for Barcelona. She joked with her old friend, Steve Engle, "It only hurts when I laugh."

Chapter Thirteen

Living Life to the Fullest

For those who knew her well, Margie and laughter became almost one. She told jokes with the best of them and her "skits on horses" (costume classes) always were filled with good humor. Perhaps it was her smiling face that made her so approachable. Not only did she sign autographs for hours on end, she continued to answer all her fans: young and old.

She remembered how appreciative she felt when the experienced riders mentored or acknowledged her. She was particularly grateful to Joe Fargis and Conrad Homfield. Joe had won Olympic Team and Individual Gold Medals in 1984, a Silver Team Medal in the following 1988 Olympics, as well as a Gold Medal in the 1975 Pan Am Games and a Fourth in the World Cup of 1989. Conrad Homfield had won Olympic Team Gold and Individual Silver. They and others offered her encouragement and kind words when she was just starting out. Margie welcomed the opportunity to "give back" and went out of her way to be helpful to the junior riders. She never hesitated to offer a helping hand.

This ability to reach out to others was never more apparent than a winter day in 1992 when Margie received a call from the Virginia Make-a-Wish

Foundation, "Margie, we have a fifteen-year-old girl with possibly terminal cancer. Autumn Hendershot will soon undergo chemotherapy and radiation treatment. She probably will lose her leg because of this. Her wish is to meet you and Daydream. Can this be arranged?"

This simple request truly inspired Margie. Mrs. Kramer had died years earlier from bone cancer, the same disease that was now threatening Autumn. "Mom, Dad, I feel as if my life has come full circle. Mrs. Kramer helped me so much. Now I can return some—" She paused to regain control. "You know what I mean. I can't believe how brave Autumn is! Even facing the amputation of her leg, she's determined to continue riding in spite of it. She's just amazing!"

Margie planned the day carefully. Autumn had pictures taken with Daydream and then Margie asked if she'd like to ride him. Autumn's eyes opened wide. "I've got posters of him. I've seen him on TV. I can't believe this!"

But that wasn't the only planned event. "Autumn, I'd like you to meet some special people who think you're pretty terrific. These two good-looking men are World Class riders, Michael Matz and Greg Best, and this pretty little gal is Julie Krone. She's the only woman jockey to ever win one of the prestigious Triple Crown races—the Belmont Stakes." Autumn looked from one rider to another and managed to give each one a little nod and a wider smile with each acknowledgement.

Later in the year, Margie and several of the other riders surprised the young equestrienne with the purchase of a horse Autumn had long admired. As they watched this courageous young girl master both her physical challenges and the readjustment of her riding technique to accommodate the prosthesis, they too felt elated by her success. As for us, when we read Mrs. Beck's (Autumn's mother) letter to our daughter, we had difficulty seeing the words through our tears. "Margie," Mrs. Beck wrote, "Your kindness and positive attitude have done so much toward helping my daughter go into remission."

Like the champions they are, each rider—Margie and Autumn—continue to admire and encourage the other.

Margie was also so impressed with the Make-a-Wish Foundation that she arranged for all the profits of her poster sales to be donated to this organization. The demand for these horse and rider pictures surprised us. Irv and I watched adults and children stand in line while Margie for as long as two, often three, hours signed her posters and spent time talking and laughing with her fans. Co-workers and friends asked us as well to intercede for them when they wanted these momentos.

"My niece is having a quince. Any chance of getting an autographed copy of Margie's poster?"

"My son's best friend thinks Margie is one gutsy lady. He saw her ride with three broken ribs. Can her inscription read 'To David' and we'll surprise him at his graduation?"

"My grandparents follow Margie on ESPN, and watched her become the first rider ever to place first, second, third, fourth, and fifth in a single Grand Prix class. I'd like a poster for Christmas."

There were also appearances on local and national television that brought their own share of surprises. After an interview with Joan Lunden on *Good Morning, America*, Margie was delighted to hear her special request. "My daughter is a huge fan of yours. She was so impressed when you won *thirteen* Grand Prix in a single season. She'd be thrilled if we made a tape right now with your wishing her a happy bat mitzvah."

*   *   *

After a big show in Palm Beach, we expected Margie's report. When a phone call came from Steve, instead of her, I could barely breathe. The strain in his voice placed us immediately on guard. "Are you both there?" He struggled for the words. "Please...don't worry. Margie is conscious now, but...but...we almost lost her in the ambulance...her heart stopped beating." My legs buckled under me, and I sank into a nearby chair. I heard Irv struggling for control, asking for the details. Shock kept us from remembering too much about the conversation, but we learned that a horse had fallen with her, stepped on her chest and back, yet miraculously she was still alive.

We entered her room. A humongous stuffed bear dominated the bed. The heavy scent of roses, gloxinias, and many mixed floral arrangements mingled with the smell of disinfectant. Gaily-colored balloons rose like silent sentinels in the midst of the animated group of visiting friends. When we finally had her all to ourselves, we asked, "Okay, Margie, how do you *really* feel?"

"Well, it only hurts when I breathe."

"What does the doctor say?"

"Several ribs are broken and several more are cracked. The stitches start in the middle of my back and continue to the middle of my front. He said I must not ride for six months."

At the end of one month and a half, Margie returned to show jumping.

"Please tell us you're entering fewer Grand Prix competitions."

"Mom, Dad, I'm doing what I feel I must." We had learned long ago when to retreat. Gradually, the look of pain left her eyes and the weekly reports filled once again with tales of successful shows and future plans.

"Dad, how much money do I have available? Can you and Mom come up to West Palm Beach on Sunday? I want you to see some property I'm looking at. Steve has already seen it and thinks it's great."

"You sound excited. What's going on?"

"Hopefully, there's going to be a *real* Gladewinds Farm, not just one on paper."

*   *   *

We were in the midst of the holiday whirl of 1994 when Margie and Steve came for a special visit. Our beaming daughter waltzed in, held up her left hand, and showed us the beautiful diamond-and-gold symbol of their engagement. "We knew you'd want to know as soon as possible."

A grinning Steve added, "I know you think it's been a long time coming, but some things are worth waiting for."

We looked at the radiant pair before us, nodded our agreement, then Irv and I hugged, kissed, and congratulated them. When the initial excitement subsided, I added, "Margie is a lot more patient than I'd have been, but we can't imagine a better choice. Steve, you're everything we would want for Margie, and we welcome you as another son."

That year, Chanukah for us, Christmas for Steve's parents, we had a particularly happy celebration. Throughout the sixteen years that Margie and Steve had known each other, the two sets of parents had much to say about the status of their children's relationship. We called Mary and Rudy Engle, who were then living in Texas, and the four of us joked about the "longest courtship on record."

Mary remarked, "I was getting ready to light a fire under that son of ours. What took them so long!"

I didn't argue. "I'd have been long gone, but Margie has more patience than I. She thinks no one on this planet measures up to your son."

Plans for the wedding began. "How many additions does that make?" The list grew with every passing day. "Margie, we don't even recognize some of these names. Who are they?"

"I know. Steve and I are beginning to feel overwhelmed. My clients and some of the people who attend the circuit are telling us they plan to show up at our wedding—invited or not."

When the list seemed destined to reach five hundred guests, the apprehensive couple approached us. "What if we just eloped?"

Our reply came quickly, "You know how long we've waited for this!"

"That's what we thought too. No, we were talking about an elopement of just our closest friends and family. Look at this brochure of Grand Cayman Island. Doesn't it look like a perfect place for a wedding? And you know everybody. We'll all have a great time."

At first the idea seemed slightly bizarre, but so did the thought of a sit-down dinner for five hundred people. "Okay, Margie and Steve, you've convinced us. We'll have an island wedding and a separate wedding reception here in Miami where we've already paid a deposit."

We renewed our efforts to find a qualified official, photographers, music, and a suitable site for the ceremony and the celebration. Our anxious bride-to-be asked, "Do you have a place reserved?"

I answered, "Well, we went to the Caymans' Chamber of Commerce here in Miami. They gave us several names, but we can't always reach them by phone."

The next time we saw Margie, she was lugging a large package. "What's this?" Irv inquired.

"I thought maybe you could fax the places easier than trying to call them," came the helpful reply. We sent out inquiries. We received pictures, prices, menus, maps and brochures by return mail. And just to be sure, I called the Department of Records at the federal courthouse to make certain the ceremony was legal in the United States.

Now came the time for the wedding dress. Margie's pupil, horse owner, and now friend, Leah Allen, had made clothes shopping easy for her. Because she was as petite as Margie, when Leah would see something she thought would be pretty or needed, she'd buy it and be reimbursed by Margie. Our daughter, so skilled in the horse arena, was totally inept when it came to a lady's dress salon.

Sherry, who would be the Matron of Honor, knew how much her best friend hated shopping, so she made an appointment for both of them to buy their dresses. While she cut my hair at her Dixie Highway beauty salon, Shear Limit, she recounted the experience. "Your daughter is impossible! She tried on one dress and said, 'That's it.' I practically forced her to try on two more. The third one looked so spectacular, everyone in the store came to admire her. I had to run back to my shop, so I left her to buy shoes on her own."   "Sherry, thank goodness for you and Leah. She'd be in rags if we left it up to her to buy clothes. And, speaking of you and Leah, the two of you are great party planners. Between her elegant shower and your nautical day in the middle of Biscayne Bay, this is becoming quite a festive occasion."

"They're such a terrific couple. I can't wait to see them married already! You and Irv must be counting the days."

"We are! We are!" But I almost missed the entire wedding.

For one week prior to our plane's departure, I lay in bed, alternately soaked in perspiration or shaking with chills. "Irv, how am I going to pack for tomorrow? I can barely move!"

"I've called your doctor. Let's see what he can do to help."

And help he did. He told me I was over the worst and gave me medication to keep my nose unclogged for the flight the following day. By the time we reached the hotel in the Grand Caymans, I could feel my strength returning.

With the arrival of each guest, the level of excitement rose. Depending on interest and temperament, adults and children selected activities of their choice. The athletes in the group, spurred by Steve's love of water sports, selected snorkelling, parasailing, and scuba diving. The sightseers explored the island on land or on sea. And, for those of us who simply wanted to rest or recuperate, the beaches and lagoons beckoned. When we all came together, everyone had a story to tell.

We met often. Margie and Steve invited the group to the Comedy Club for Friday evening. The comedians had a field day with the couple who had first dated seventeen years prior, but in response Margie replied with a reasonably straight face, "We don't believe in rushing into anything."

Mary and Rudy Engle's rehearsal dinner the next evening took place in a green, tropical paradise. Everywhere we looked, we saw graceful palms and fragrant frangipani trees bordered with multihued impatiens. Sunday morning, Nancy and Ed Pastroff, Dee and Wally Berman hosted the wedding guests at a relaxed, bountiful buffet brunch in the hotel's main dining room. Dee had brought disposable cameras for the family, and the constant flashing added a light dimension to the occasion.

Saturday afternoon, Irv and I took a taxi to check on the restaurant that we had selected long distance. The building did not look as pretty as the pictures, but the food at lunch reminded us that we had based our selection on the international reputation of the chef. The wedding was set for the next day, Sunday, 5:00 P.M., November 18, 1995.

One hour prior to the wedding, our suite buzzed with activity. Sherry came over to help Margie with her hair. Margie was rearranging our carefully worked-out seating plan. The taxi was late and we were running out of time. Irv called the taxi company only to find out other guests had taken the first cab. He ordered a second car and, wanting no more hijacks, arranged to meet them in a hidden alley behind the hotel.

I turned around to check on Margie. My eyes misted. "You look…you look…absolutely gorgeous." Her brown eyes sparkled. Her normally light-brown hair was flecked with sun-bleached gold. Her form-fitting, white satin and pearl-encrusted lace, ankle-length dress hugged her curves smoothly, then flared out in a graceful swirl. She wore a shoulder-length veil, my borrowed earrings, and the traditional—but hidden—blue garter.

Suddenly, I began to laugh. "Margie, what are you doing?"

Realizing that she could not walk in her unaccustomed high-heeled shoes, she was busy stuffing tissues into the toes of the oversized footwear. "I guess I should have tried them on before buying them. I just hate taking the time to shop."

Sherry looked over and shrugged her shoulders. "I told you she was impossible!"

The taxi finally arrived, and we rushed to our designated area in the restaurant. "Irv, what happened to this old building? It's lovely—positively aglow with the sun's reflection."

We looked outside from a hidden porch in the restaurant. Margie was smiling. "I can't believe how beautiful everything is! Thank you both."

A delicate white gazebo had been set up on one side of the pier under the wild pines. Steve, his best man Jim Kenney, and the clergyman were waiting there. Behind them, the guests already were seated with an aisle left open for our upcoming walk. We could hear the music faintly over the sound of the ocean lapping at the large rocks below the pier. And the sky! The sky's horizon blazed red, pink, and orange hues as the setting sun's reflection danced upon the blue and gold water.

"I don't think any one of us will forget this beautiful place, but look at your groom, Margie. He looks a little worried." Steve's strong, handsome face was strained with concern for our late arrival. He pushed up the sleeves of his island-formal white shirt to look at his watch.

Mark and Eddie had seen us arrive and were waiting to lead me to my seat. I placed a hand into each of my son's arms and looked at their familiar, well-loved faces. "How lucky I am to be escorted by the two best-looking men on the island!"

We took our seats and turned to watch the rest of the wedding party. Suzi, our nine-year-old little granddaughter, looked like a younger version of her Aunt Margie. She dropped her rose pedals carefully along the path, walked slowly down the aisle, and then joined her parents. She looked relieved that her part was over. Next came Sherry, radiant in her flowered, festive dress. Just before the bride and her father stepped into the aisle, we heard the swelling notes of the wedding march. Margie smiled broadly, but the mixture of many complex feelings flitted across Irv's face.

The ceremony pleased the families of both religions. The clergyman, a Universalist, spoke of the love and the similar virtues that bound Steve and Margie. His elegant British accent served as a reminder that the Caymans were a part of Great Britain, as did their marriage certificate we read later. Dr. and Mrs. Steven Engle were now husband and wife by order of Her Royal Majesty, Queen Elizabeth II.

When the reverend announced "You may kiss the bride," a well-timed breeze lifted Margie's veil from her face and over her head. Every time we viewed the video, she would say, "Watch! Isn't that amazing? I can't believe the wind did that!"

Chef Tell enhanced his reputation with the dinner that followed the ceremony. Steve was delighted. "I've been in many places and many countries, but this is the single best meal I've ever had." Margie, too excited to eat her entire meal, had it wrapped for the following day. The guests toasted and teased the happy couple well into the night.

Everyone agreed. The honeymooners had succeeded in their hope that the Goldstein and Engle families and closest friends would really get to know one another and that each guest would enjoy and remember their unusual wedding celebration and vacation.

When they returned, Margie moved her residence to Steve's. But the two of them continued to travel back and forth between Wellington and North Miami, their work-related barns, the out-of-town sites that comprised the show-jumping circuit plus the race tracks where Steve began at daybreak. We could not help worrying. "It sure would be great if the two of you could slow down. You look so tired."

Also, Steve was attending classes to acquire additional training in acupuncture and chiropractic medicine for large animals. Margie proudly told us how successful these skills were. "Steve went to one of his owner's barn. T.P. was in such pain, he reared whenever Steve tried to touch him. Steve got two others to hold the horse while he began the chiropractic manipulation. In the middle of T.P.'s struggles, he suddenly realized he was *not* hurting and placed his head on Steve's shoulder. You could almost hear him saying 'Hey! That feels great.' The next time Steve went to the barn, T.P. ran in from the pasture and put his head on Steve's shoulder. Who says horses can't talk?"

Not only did Margie benefit from these services, but other riders did as well. Steve found himself flying to more and more "horse/house calls" when his wife was on the circuit and driving to the numerous barns where Margie had rented stalls for her owner's horses.

In an effort to relieve some of the complications in their lives, Margie turned to family and friends for time she just didn't have. "Dad, would you work out the finances to see how much we can invest in Gladewinds?" "Alan, thanks for loaning me your secretary and for expediting the legalities!" "Leah, thanks for taking care of my clothes shopping."

After a few years of frustrations, setbacks, and some financial assistance from the family, the barn became a reality. When we first walked through the brand-new, beautiful building with its thirty stalls and attached apartment for the horses' grooms, we gazed in wonder. The burnt-orange clay tiles spread protectively over the roof. The green shutters opened wide to let the horses enjoy the cool breezes. Gazing through two of the windows were our old veterans from the early days, Saluut and Daydream, now living a life of leisurely retirement. The floors and white walls were spotless. Newly-painted white fencing surrounded ten acres of leveled land. A brightly-colored sign proclaimed to one and all, "Gladewinds Farm/ Margie Goldstein Engle, Owner."

Sherry and her little four-year-old daughter, Brittani, had taken the tour with us. Her eyes filled with delight for her friend and she inquired, "Did you ever think you'd see this day?"

I shook my head, unable to answer. My thoughts had drifted back to Dorothy Kramer and how proud she would be. "Gladewinds will live forever, Margie, because I'm *giving* the name to you. I know you'll never bring anything but honor to it."

Chapter Fourteen

Glory Days

As the weekly wins accumulated, the yearly standings rose as well.

Annually and with great pleasure, the Goldstein friends and families listened to the Palm Beach or Tampa show-jumping announcer intone:

"Can you believe it? Only Gold Medal World Champion (1986) Katie Monahan Prudent has been Rider of the Year three times. With this AGA 1994 win, Margie Goldstein joins the masters!"

"Ladies and Gentlemen, Margie Goldstein Engle has broken another record. Our clear winner for the 1995 AGA Rider of the Year is now taking her victory gallop around the course."

"The last rider, the first clear round! Ladies and Gentlemen, there will be no jump-off. Margie Goldstein Engle, the first four-time winner is now the first *five*-time AGA Rider of the Year!"

This five-time feat has been unmatched in the history of the sport. 1989, 1991, 1994, 1995, 1996—the American GrandPrix Association can be very proud of this true champion. In later years, she would break still more records and earn additional AGA Rider of the Year Awards.

"Well, little sister, who would have thought it? National Grand Prix League Rider of the Year Award for three years, the Hertz Equestrian of the Year Award, now this! Do you have any more surprises up your sleeve?"

"Just this one. Happy Birthday, Eddie! I won the Rolex Grand Prix in Germantown, and I've been saving this watch for you. I hope you like it."

The guests at the Goldstein dinner table laughed. "You should see your face, Ed. You seem a little startled."

"I've been admiring yours and Steve's watches, Margie, but I never expected to have a Rolex of my own."

"What kind of wife and sister would I be if I couldn't keep you both in good times?"

"Margie," groaned her nephew, Matt. "Good *times*? You can do better than that."

"Speaking of good times, I've been reorganizing some of the family pictures. Let's go enjoy them," I offered.

Margie's nephew, Jeff, looked through the album and commented, "Well, Grandma, I'm glad to see you've got all our school snapshots up to date."

Suzi had already flipped back to the photographs of the entire family when Margie and Steve had married in the Grand Caymans. "Oh, that was so much *fun*!"

*   *   *   *   *

The wins are so easy to accept; the losses must be borne with grace. Margie started 1996 with a herniated disk in a spine so filled with pain that, for several weeks, she was barely able to move, much less to compete. Although two doctors urged surgery, Dr. Brown at Jackson Memorial Hospital was that rare surgeon who didn't immediately use a scalpel as the first solution. "Margie, the bed rest you were forced to take was something your body desperately needed. Now I want you to try these exercise techniques." He handed her a list. "You really should give up horse riding, because the constant pounding on your vertebrae is not helping the curvature in your spine."

Margie started to interrupt, but Dr. Brown continued. "I've already heard you'll compete no matter what I say, so we'll order a back brace that you must wear when you ride and when you feel the first signs of pain." Margie followed his directions carefully and returned to successful competition.

*   *   *

We met two of Margie's owners who took great pride in the quality of their stables. I remember being introduced to Ben Al Saud, a member of the royal family of Saudi Arabia, and his entourage. He was short, darkly good looking, with a vividly-hued parrot on his shoulder named appropriately "Colors." By his side stood a tall beautiful blonde. Behind him was his truck—the most colorful I had ever seen. Cumulus clouds were painted above a sky-blue background. Mounted hurdle-jumping horses that Margie rode for him had been airbrushed to match Ben's image. In large multi-hued letters were painted, "Rainbow Farms." He graciously took us to see his favorite horses: Land Of Kings, a 17-hand white stallion and Caribbean Queen, a 17-hand Westphalian bloodbay mare.

"Margie, considering the situation in the Mid East, how do you and Ben get along?"

She ignored my implications. "Other riders have asked me that. We started out with distinct and differing opinions about many things, including the treatment of the horses. But we've learned to accommodate one another."

"How is that?"

"Now that he has confidence in me, I do the training, decide how many times the horses will enter—I don't want the horses too tired—and what classes each is capable of. He continues to warm up the horses just before we show them, but only on the flat and only a couple of jumps."

"That's it?"

"Some of the riders are more conservative and they laugh when we go in the ring. Ben likes gaudy saddle pads, leg wrappings in rainbow colors and multi-colored reins. They tell me that there's no way they'd ride his 'carousel horses.' Yet many of the people who come to see us want to take pictures of me atop one of Ben's steeds. They *love* the flashy effect!"

When Ben was killed in the New York airplane crash of 1998, Margie mourned the loss of a close and valued friend.

We met Mike Polaski, a tall, muscular horse-owner, imposing in his all black outfit, at one of the shows in Tampa. "Tell us about Mike, Honey. He seems to be quiet, but taking in everything."

"Mike runs a successful insurance business—Specialty Underwriters, Inc.—in Wisconsin. He's always been interested in horses and has a beautiful—impeccable taste—stable there where he's hoping to breed jumpers, not hunters, at the top level. I met him a few years ago—about 1990 or '91—at a horse show in Wisconsin. He's had several trainers before me, but the horses they bought for him weren't competitive enough for Mike."

"How so?"

"He runs the stable, Hidden Creek, as a business—buying and selling, but he wants a strong string of horses that can compete at the Grand Prix level. He's willing to do what it takes to have a quality string while he's waiting for his own horses to breed Grand Prix horses. And he really takes an active interest in the competition, watching often no matter where we travel. Also, he likes to decide which horse will be competing."

As we watched Margie ride Hidden Creek's Alvaretto and Hidden Creek's Laurel, two of his recent purchases, we marvelled at their strength and grace that indicated excellent potential.

*   *   *

In June of '96 with Olympic competition almost complete and Caribbean Queen in second spot for one of the top four positions, a despondent Margie called. "Mom, Dad, would you believe lightning just struck for the second time?"

"Margie, are you alright? We can barely hear you."

Her voice sounded flat and low. "Remember when Saluut's leg was injured just before the Olympic trials?"

"That's not something we're likely to forget! Oh, Lord! What happened?"

"In the horse van on the way to the show, Caribbean Queen injured her leg. For me there will be no Olympics. I..I just can't believe it."

What irony! Here was Margie, ranked number one in the United States, but unable to represent her country in the most exciting and well-known event in the world. "Oh, Honey. I wish we could help. You've dreamed of this for so long."

"I know. The Europeans think we're crazy. Their national equestrian committees simply identify their four outstanding riders and one alternate. They say we wear out our horses by having an intense period of elimination during the trials. But.." Her voice trailed off.

Yet, if there are disappointments in sports, there are times to celebrate. Margie had competitive horses she loved and who were anxious to jump. In 1996, she rode Mike's Holsteiner chestnut gelding, Hidden Creek's Alvaretto, to the number one position: AGA Horse of the Year. She described Al as a little horse (16 hands) that thinks he's big. "He's quick and careful, compact and feisty—a spunky little gutsy horse who loves to jump."

And, just to ensure the pleasure, she rode Hidden Creek's Laurel right behind him to the number two spot: 1996 AGA Reserve Champion of the Year. In the AHSA standing, she rode Laurel to the number one position with Alvaretto closing in as Reserve Champion. Margie describes Laurel as "…the most consistent horse I've ever known. She holds the record for the most first-round clean rounds, for the AGA and all events, with 17 in a row, and that included many of the nation's toughest shows."

When he accompanied his horses to the Winner's Circle at the AGA final event in Palm Beach, the owner of Hidden Creek Farm, Mike Polaski—hardly the quiet man we had first thought him to be—bubbled over with pride!

In 1997 Margie qualified to represent the United States in Italy, Switzerland, the Netherlands, France, and Germany. Both Steve and Mike were there to cheer her on, and she didn't disappoint them. The Grand Prix and Leading Rider international events added up to her computer ranking as the Leading Lady Rider in the World. The 1998 World Cup in Helsinki clinched it when Margie won several events during the week and narrowly missed the number one position at the final Grand Prix. In fact, Margie held the title of the World's Leading Lady Rider for 115 weeks— a record to be proud of.

Upon hearing about the Helsinki win, her brother Eddie said, "That's the first time I remember Margie being satisfied with second place."

"But, Ed, the second leading rider at the World Cup Finals plus winning many classes at the same show? Well, I'd say that was satisfying, *very* satisfying indeed!"

Also, Margie and her teammates brought home the silver medal from the 1999 Pan American games in Winnepeg, Canada, thereby qualifying the United States to participate in Olympics 2000. *Jewish Women* magazine featured her as one of the top ten women in the world for the year 5760 (1999-2000). Margie was so far ahead in the computer rankings for her *sixth* AGA Rider of the Year (1999) Award that the programs in both Palm Beach and Tampa featured her on the cover and in their contents before the final event on April 8, 2000. I looked at the cover on the Tampa program and noted, "Irv, will you look at that? The cover shot of Margie features one very large, very black eye!"

One of Margie's fans taped the Grand Prix in Rome. Although all the announcing was in Italian, every now and then we heard our daughter's name. The camera panned the stands as an estimated thirty-five thousand people enthusiastically supported their favorite riders. They loudly cheered as the jump-off of the few competitors with clear rounds narrowed down to only one show jumper. We had no trouble recognizing three words from the announcer: Margie Goldstein Engle.

The Star-Spangled Banner never sounded so stirring or so beautiful to our ears as at that moment when the camera focused upon our daughter's smiling face and the flag of our United States superimposed behind her image. I commented to Irv, "Gee, I wish I could understand what they're saying."

I agreed with his reply. " Sometimes words are not necessary."

*   *   *

Acclaim, accident, triumph, tragedy. Would we ever get used to the pattern?

"Margie, are you alright now? How did it happen?"

"I can't believe I was so stupid. It had rained so badly, I withdrew my horses from the competition. I didn't want them to be hurt. But one of the horses we sold to a junior rider was giving his new owner problems and I was trying to iron out the kinks. When the horse skidded suddenly because of the wet ground, I was thrown into the metal cups on the jump."

"The *metal* cups?" Please, I can't bear it—what happened!"

"My nose was splayed open. Fortunately, the doctor on call was able to put me back together. He used thirty-six stitches to sew up my nose and lip. Steve watched him and said he was very good."

"How horrible! You weren't able to compete in the World Championship Trials the following day."

"Well…"

"Oh, Margie, how could you?"

"I was able to have a clear first round, but my eyes were swollen almost shut and I was in such pain that I just did okay in the jump off."

When we saw both the accident and Margie's mangled face on the delayed broadcasts, we could barely contain our tears. Steve insisted that she come home for time to recover; but, during those weeks in the summer of '98, we found looking at Margie painful.

*   *   *

"Margie, we're going to be in Australia and New Zealand besides stopping in L.A. to see Mark, Cindy, and the kids. It will be the longest time we've ever been away, so Dad will need to prepare your payroll information in advance."

"When is this?"

"We'll be gone all the month of April."

"Then you'll miss the 1999 American Invitational."

"It's usually in March. What happened? Cousin Sue has already let us know our room is ready and waiting for us."

"This may be the last year it's in Tampa. The date was changed."

"Oh, Honey, we're so sorry. We always have such a good time there. Perhaps it's just as well. We haven't brought you much luck."

"Maybe it's because this particular event means so much to me. I've been going to Tampa—just to watch—since I was a little girl, and my dream was to be able to ride in the Invitational and one day be the winner."

"You've come close. Remember when you rode a perfect round and your horse missed going through the exit time sensor? The judges counted it as a refusal."

"How could I forget!"

We were in the middle of an Australian rain forest in a small hotel called Silky Oaks when Margie's fax arrived. She had copied the *Tampa Tribune* article describing the event and written across the top, "At last!"

Ah, the wonders of technology! In this remote little place half way around the world, we were able to share her news.

When we arrived home in Miami, we watched the televised event, still being broadcast at several scheduled times. We knew the stress and thrill that each rider felt. *The American Invitational* is a prestigious and exciting Grand Prix for the thirty riders selected. Because the event is by invitation only, there is no entry fee for the competitors. The riders are limited to only one horse, so they make their selection carefully.

Course designer Steve Stephens crafted his hurdles with full knowledge of the competence at this level. He arranged thirteen varied and colorful obstacles of five feet or more in height with one double combination and one triple, requiring sixteen jumps total. His triple combination was particularly difficult, because the first and third jumps included a seven-foot spread within the two-fenced oxers. The middle element in the triple included visual barriers designed to fool and confuse a horse in motion. Because Mr. Stephens was among those who thought horses are color blind, he had the top part painted white, thus fading the poles into the background, and the bottom part painted blue with a distracting water hazard underneath. Following the thirteenth obstacle, a liverpool (an extra-wide water hazard) reflected the glare of the flood lights at the evening event. This can, and does, spook the horses.

"Get your programs here. Only five dollars." Members of the Tampa area Pony Clubs happily hawked their official information magazines to the gathering spectators.

The cavernous new stadium gleamed in readiness. The air was crisp and comfortable; and, above the stands, the large American flag fluttered in the breeze. At each end of the bowl, two huge television screens provided clear coverage and instant replay or extended coverage of this much-heralded event. A mammoth pirate ship with its pioneer pier homes and warehouses dominated the entire west side of the stadium and served as a reminder of Tampa's early history. A column of mounted police, two abreast, paraded onto the field with the American flags they carried whipping in the breeze. The stage was set.

Margie had alternately tested and rested Hidden Creek's Alvaretto prior to this competition and felt he was equal to the task. As she walked the course with the other riders, she planned her strategy. Many sports writers have described her as one of the most cerebral strategists, and she had no intention of disappointing them or herself. Her advantage would be that she had earned the right to ride close to the end. (Riders go in reverse order of their current standings.) Her disadvantage would be that she would be followed by three of the nation's most outstanding riders.

Twenty-four attempts preceded her. One rider voluntarily withdrew when his horse twice refused the number-ten fence. One rider thrilled the crowd with her clear round, but exceeded the time allowance of ninety-three seconds, for a quarter of a point penalty. The others disassembled one or more of the jumps. As expected, most of these knocked-down fences occurred within the triple combination. The excited fans cheered the valiant efforts and groaned with each falling rail.

Margie and Alvaretto entered the arena to a roaring welcome. His brushed chestnut body gleamed under the floodlights. His head swung from side to side, his eyes bulged far from their sockets, making him appear to be fighting Margie's control. As he burst over the first fence, broadcaster Lysa Burke chuckled and announced, "Al is dancing tonight." Margie, knowing that Alvaretto sometime got nervous, settled him down, trying to maintain an easy but steady gait. "Okay, Al, easy does it. Everything will be fine."

They turned to approach the fourth obstacle, an airy, three-panelled vertical, designed to confuse the horse and make the rider quickly select the middle of one of the series of three poles. They cleared this penalty-producing fence. "Good boy, you're doing great!"

Margie took a fast peek at the time as they rode to the eighth obstacle. This brightly-hued butterfly standard measured over six and one-half feet, taller than either rider or steed. They cleared this and counted the paces to the Seaworld obstacle with its heavy planks balanced precariously on flat cups. The slightest tap caused the plank to drop, and several competitors heard the thud as they jumped over it. Margie steered her talented stallion upward. "I knew you could do it! Great, great, great Alvaretto!"

On to the triple combination and not one sound could be heard from the spectators. When she cleared the last element, the buzzing began. As Margie and Alvaretto sailed over fences twelve and thirteen, the roar of the standing crowd erupted with a life of its own.

After her fault-free round, we listened to the interviewer ask her, "Only once in the history of the American Invitational has a rider won without a jump-off. What do you think your chances are to do the same?"

Her reply was realistic. "We have three riders at the top of their form coming up. Any one of them could easily overtake me."

Allison Firestone and Gustil P, an excellent duo, dropped a fence early in the round, but recovered to become the fastest of the riders with four faults. Nona Garson, equally talented, and her often-winning partner, Rhythmical, had trouble from the beginning, but continued their efforts. As they approached the middle element in the triple combination, the reflected light spooked Rhythmical and he refused the jump. Nona was thrown from her horse, expertly landed on her feet, and withdrew from the competition.

McLain Ward, 1998 Rider of the Year and the previous year's winner, entered the arena. Margie felt the camera upon her and tried hard to keep her expression neutral. McLain rode smoothly and well until he attempted the treacherous triple combination. When the pole hit the ground, the announcer's voice was drowned out over the crowd's cheering for Margie. We heard Lysa over the noise in the stadium. "Finally! It couldn't happen to a nicer person."

We couldn't agree more!

Chapter Fifteen

Going for the Gold

The year 1999 continued with one win after another. Margie earned her sixth AGA Rider of the Year with ease. Still she worried about the horses. Even though she tried to alternately compete, then rest, her mounts; she could tell some were not going to be ready physically for the Olympic Trials coming up the following year. No matter how well riders planned, injuries created their own timelines.

She discussed the situation with the owner of Hidden Creek Farms. "Mike, what would you think about buying another horse of Grand Prix caliber? Both Laurel and Al are still capable, but Laurel's taking a lot longer to recover than we thought, and Al is getting older and needs more time between his many trials. Since next year will be a grueling one with the Olympics and all, we might be better off with a new one I saw."

Mike listened to Margie's critique, the pros and cons of each horse she had considered. "Our best bet might be Perin. He moves like an athlete, is scopey and careful, but the owner is asking a high price for an inexperienced horse. He had planned to show him, but he never did."

"Isn't that the horse you told me about last year?"

"Yes, but even then, the owner was asking too high a price. Perin's large—he stands tall at 17. 1 ½ hands—and he likes to jump."

"If that's what you think, then go for it!"

Margie felt enormous gratitude for her supportive owner and friend. "I think he's got a lot of talent."

Irv and I saw Hidden Creek's Perin for the first time at the Palm Beach 2000 circuit. He was bay colored, of Westphalian lineage, and he looked enormous. After several performances, I said, "Irv, he looks awfully green to me. How many Sundays have we seen him show? He'll be going great and then—down comes a fence."

"Well, Margie has faith in him. That's what's important."

What she didn't tell us was how unfit he was when he arrived from Germany. We *read* about him in an interview in which Margie was quoted. "We just got him out of quarantine and I am telling everyone how much I like this horse. So he gets here and he is so out of shape and his feet are so bad. I'm telling everyone how great he is and the poor horse couldn't trot once around the ring without gasping for breath! I couldn't jump him at first, and then I took him to the Gold Cup, and luckily Mike wasn't there to see this poor horse. When Mike showed up, he wasn't too impressed, because Perin's not even near what I had tried two years earlier. He had done nothing! Was too unfit to hack—let alone jump!"

There was a large show at the Miami Arena and two equally large events in Tampa. We attended them with the hope of seeing progress from this large, friendly horse. Irv commented, "Well, Perin is the best of the four-faulters."

"Remember what you told me? Margie has faith in him. She says he's very consistent for this level and we have to remember his lack of experience."

The Olympic 2000 Trials began in the last week of June in Gladstone, New Jersey. We were happy that Steve would be with her both for moral support and to take care of the horses. He promised to call us the minute each trial was over.

After the first event on Wednesday, Steve's voice boomed across the wires. "Do you want to know who was the *only* clear rider today?"

My words came tumbling out. "Are you telling us what I think you are?"

"That's right. Perin rode beautifully on the most difficult course I've ever seen. Your daughter will be busy signing autographs for hours, so she'll talk to you later."

When we got off the phone, Irv and I both began exclaiming to one another. "I-I-I think this is wonderful."

"Easy does it, Mona. There's a long way to go."

On Friday, Steve called in the morning, then later that afternoon. "She's still number one! Margie is the only rider with three fault-free rounds."

"Great! Great! Great! Thank you so much for keeping us posted, Steve. And we promised to let Mark and Eddie and the rest of the family know, so we'll relay the news here and to L.A. That's just wonderful!"

On Saturday, Steve called again. "Steve, why are you calling? Is everything alright?"

He laughed. "We're in Detroit, and Margie just won the Grand Prix tonight on Reggae. Boy, is she on a roll! Just as soon as the rain stops, we're headed back to New Jersey."

Later that evening, I said to Irv, "I know I must be the world's biggest worry wart, but I sure wish they were back in Gladstone *safely*."

Sunday morning crawled slowly as we imagined what was going on in Gladstone. Finally, the phone rang. "Mark?"

"I wondered if you knew what was happening. I've searched through the Internet and I can't find how Margie did."

"What do you mean? Steve will call with the results."

"The Internet lists everyone who competed in the Trial Four show jumping event and their scores. I've read every name. I can't find Margie's. "

My thoughts leaped ahead. "Oh no, she didn't get back in time for the trials."

I could hear Mark's shock which now matched our own. Irv said, "We can't stay on the phone. Steve is probably trying to call."

The next couple of hours were sheer torture. First, her dad and I worried that Margie and Steve had been delayed by the weather and had never made it back to the Trials. "She'll be out—no Olympics. Not again. I can't believe this."

I tried to distract myself with a book, but I kept reading the same paragraph over and over and was unable to stay focused. Irv tried to pick up news on the Internet, but was unsuccessful. He remembered that the phone line was tied into the computer and we didn't want to miss Steve's call, so he gave up on this source. When he came into the family room to turn on the news, I feared the worse. "Do you think there was an accident?" I said silent prayers for their safety.

Long minutes turned into longer hours. "I can't stand it. I'm going to try to reach Steve."

Irv cautioned. "Bad news travels quickly. If anything happened, they'd let us know. Don't tie up the phone."

At this point, my nerves were raw. "I *must* do something. I'll call on Steve's phone."

When his telephone answering machine began the recording, I was too choked up to leave a message. Next I called on Margie's cell phone. The laughter in our son-in-law's voice as he began with "I was just going to call you." was reassuring.

"Steve, we hadn't heard from you and—of course—thought the worse. Is Margie all right? What's going on?"

"Everything is fine *now*. Perin was really scared when he twisted his shoe in the middle of Trial Four this morning, but—amazingly—he kept on going. We've been quite busy—getting everything rebuilt and putting padding between his hoof and the shoe. They allow you to drop your lowest score during these five events, so that worked out. He was still shaken up for the trial that followed this afternoon, but Margie managed to bring him under control with only 9¼ faults. She has to stay in the top four. She's now number three in the Olympic standings."

"But they're okay?"

Margie called us back later to reassure us that all was well. "Perin is so brave. I thought he had thrown his shoe, but I felt terrible when I saw it was still attached and had twisted into his hoof. But why were *you* so worried?"

I repeated the series of circumstances, then added, "Why did *you* feel you had to go to Detroit in the middle of the Olympic Trials?"

"Mom, I rode Reggae for Robert Pergement besides Mike's horses."

"Yes?"

"You know how supportive and wonderful he's been all through the years."

"But—"

"I bet you've forgotten what happened in South Hampton."

"You're right. What happened there?"

"Mr. Pergement was in the hospital recovering from an operation. I was showing his horse, Global. He got special permission from his doctor to come to the fairgrounds just so he could see us ride—good thing we won. He was so happy—went back to the hospital and told everyone that's what he needed to recover."

"But you could have missed the Trials—how could you take a chance like that?"

"I was showing some of Mike's horses also—Jones won a third. He sent his private plane when he heard that we couldn't make the commercial plane back. You didn't have to worry."

I felt arguing further was useless. "Margie, I guess that's our job as parents. What surprised us was how upset your brother was. When Mark and Cindy come to the second half of the Trials in August, you're going to have a pair of very nervous fans in the stands." Oh, did those words prove to be prophetic!

During the next several weeks, we kept the phone lines very busy. "Where are you this week, Margie?" "You're joining Margie *where*, Steve? How are you keeping up with the track and your practice?"

Steve responded, "I can't keep up. I finally had to give up the horses at the track, because of all the travels. When I'm back in Miami, I have time for only the country practice."

"Steve, I hope you feel as good about that as we do. Her dad and I feel a lot more at ease when we know Margie is with you. She told us the other riders appreciate your taking care of their horses also. You can't be in three places at once. Two's enough."

In the beginning of August, the second half of the Trials began. From 76 competitors, there were now twelve. A few days before the competition began, Allison Firestone's horse Jox developed an abscess in his foot and they had to withdraw. I didn't have to imagine how she felt. Our family had been there.

Now only eleven horse-and-rider combinations would compete. Three days. Five competitions. Perhaps it was lack of sleep. Perhaps it was nerves. We felt the mounting pressure.

Steve called after every event. Mark called after every event. After each call, I would relay the information to family and friends who had asked us to keep them informed. On Sunday, August 6, the fourth and final call came from Steve at the Del Mar Horse Park in California. He held the phone in the air, then talked into it. "Margie is in the number one position. I just wanted you two to hear the applause. That's your daughter they're cheering for!"

The family finally had a chance to celebrate later in the month. Margie had returned to regular competition with runs out to California to keep Perin exercised while he was in quarantine. She was in South Florida for only a couple of days. Eddie, Beth, and Suzi—Matt and Jeff were away at college—joined Irv and me when we met at "The King and I" in Miami Lakes for dinner. Along with its great Thai and Japanese food, this restaurant—midway between our various distances—had served (over many years) suchi and solace, sizzle and celebration.

As we toasted our successful daughter, I asked, "Margie, we've all been nervous wrecks. How have you stayed so calm?"

"There's so much to *think* about when you're riding."

Suzi looked at Margie thoughtfully. "What do you mean?"

"You have to really be in tune with the horse: aware of what's in his mind, how he's responding, where to speed up, where you have to approach cautiously. The courses for the Olympics Trials are especially tricky."

Now it was Ed's turn to ask, "How so?"

"Not only were the obstacles more difficult—wider oxers, wider water hazards, cups that barely held the rails, but the strides between hurdles were quite complicated. The course designer built half-strides added to full ones, so you really had to have good communication with your horse. You're constantly adjusting his stride, lengthening or shortening it."

"But you kept your clothes clean!" I teased.

Margie colored slightly, then looked at each of us. "You *know* I'm not superstitious. Honest!"

I felt mischievous and grinned at one and all who looked at me with no clue to this unexpected conversational reference. "I'll bet your family would love to hear about your one little pre-show ritual."

"Okay. Okay. It began with Spank. Whenever I was wearing something new, he'd pick up a little bit of dirt and rub it onto my clean clothes. Then he'd tell me: You're going to get dirty the *easy* way or the *hard* way. Let's do it the easy way. I guess it's just habit now, but I do the same thing for me and for my pupils."

I laughed, then lifted my glass. "Well, it's a nice way to remember Spank. Meanwhile, a toast: we're awfully proud of you—on and off the course! Good luck in Sydney and you and Steve, enjoy, enjoy!"

She left the following morning. We resumed visiting by phone, but the month between the conclusion of the Olympic Trials and leaving for

Sydney was hectic. I asked, "Margie, what's going on? Every time we talk to you, you're in another city and winning another Grand Prix."

"Well, I'll be in Sydney for several weeks, and I want to stay in shape. Also, I want to keep the other horses—that weren't in the trials—going. It's way too easy to get rusty."

Irv said, "We're getting phone calls from friends and relatives all over the country who have seen you in delayed broadcasts from the Hamptons or Indianapolis or Port Jervis or Boston. How are you making all these connections?"

The memory of anticipation and excitement accelerated Margie's words as they tumbled out in explanation. "When I told the officials that I couldn't get from the Grand Prix in Port Jervis to the one in Boston just a few hours later, they said they'd send a private plane and a limo for me. We got to the airport and were fogged in. We were late and the show had already started. They let the three of us—Lynn Little, Candice King and me—walk the course when the rider left the arena."

I gave her a startled reply. "Good heavens! How do you take that kind of pressure?"

Margie laughed. "I won the top spot and Lynne came in second."

Irv chimed in. "When do you leave for Sydney? How about Perin— when does he fly over?"

"Oh, I spoke to the groom, who flew with Perin. He said that, from the moment they put him in the large container, he didn't like it at all! But, if he wasn't left alone, then he was fine."

I exclaimed, "Poor guy. He just wanted company. What happened to him when he landed in Australia?'

"Once they landed, Perin went into quarantine again."

"And what about you and Steve? When do you leave?"

"I'll be leaving for L.A. in a couple of days—the USET officials will be going over the rules and expectations with the team—and Steve will follow in just a few days after that."

*   *   *

Family and friends continued to call. One of the calls that I truly cherished came from Margie's mentor.

"Hi, Mrs. Goldstein. I just wanted to let you know how thrilled we all are about your daughter. I hope you realize how terrific she is."

"Well, Karen, you've just proven why it's so great talking to you. Only kidding—I love to hear from you. I agree, but we're a little biased."

"During Marj-or-ee's last visit...."

"You still tease her with that gosh awful name?"

"And she still hates it! Anyway we had the greatest talk the last time she was here that I wanted to tell you about it."

"How were you both able to meet? She's busier than ever."

"We met at Sherry's—while we were waiting for our hair appointments, we talked and talked and talked—haven't been able to do that in years. I told her that in one way I was kind of sad. She was doing everything I had wanted to and never was able to."

"Oh, Karen....."

"No, no, it's all right. Margie reminded me that it was all a matter of choice. You've raised three wonderful children—you *chose* to do that, she said. You could have been an Olympian or gone as far as you wanted. You *chose* that path. Then she went on to ask if I could possibly regret that choice and I couldn't say I did. In fact, after I spoke to her I felt so good that she was doing this for *all* of us at Gladewinds. She's just a fine human being and you should be so proud of her, Mona."

"Karen, surely you must know that a part of *you* is going to Sydney also."

Karen laughed. "Your daughter told me those exact same words."

Another exchange that delighted both Irv and me was an e-mail from Nancy Unger Fink and her ten-year-old daughter. Nikki sent a copy of her school report, an extremely comprehensive biography of Margie that included the early days at Gladewinds Farm, the ponies Margie broke, trained and showed, her college years, and her professional history. Nikki wrote, "She became somewhat of a phenomenon. ....She is currently the best rider of Show Jumping (sic) in the history of the United States!....Margie is like the president of the country in the horse world. All horse-loving kids look up to Margie as a role moel. She is really good at writing to people that write her fan mail." Her last paragraph concluded with Margie's Olympic dreams and hopes.

I answered Nikki that, as a fourth-grade teacher, I would say she earned an A+ in every category: sentence structure, vocabulary, punctuation, creativity, organization, etc. When I teased her that the only thing she didn't include was mention of her mother's and Margie's childhood giggling, she found a way to work that into her report as well.

I'm sure it's no surprise that Nikki's composition received a prominent position in the scrapbook I'm making for Margie.

*   *   *

The trip for Margie and Steve was equally long and tedious; but, from the moment of arrival, the sense of place and pleasure never left them. Two years earlier, Irv and I encountered only fun-loving, gracious Australians in our travels through their country. The Engles, as guests of the host Olympic country, met (as they told us later) "the most happy, helpful, friendly, and efficient people in the history of the planet. Everyone greeted us with 'G'day ' and—when we say everyone—there are thousands and thousands of volunteers who made everything so easy and so delightful for all the Olympians. The merchants gave us magic coins to use in the vending machines. We not only got our selected items, but our coins boomeranged back as well. Their hospitality tents included food for every nationality and it was all free!"

Along with the rest of the Olympic equestrian and rowing teams and support personnel, Steve and Margie were housed in a little country town called Penrith to be nearer to their competitive venues. When they drove into Sydney, twenty-five miles away, they carefully dodged the numerous kangaroos. Cute as these unique-to-Australia animals were, they presented a formidable obstacle to the newly-arrived visitors who had to navigate around them. Even the native Australians drove with special bumpers to avoid hitting the 'roos.

The day after the inspiring, spirited Opening Ceremonies, Margie and Steve spoke to an oarsman on the Netherlands Team. "Wow, were we pumped up! We couldn't believe how exciting this would be. We were driving here and—out of the blue—this giant animal appeared in our headlights. We stopped the car and there's this kangaroo—we'd hit him— and we felt badly, but what could we do? My buddy decides he's got to have a picture of this. So he takes off the jacket of his uniform, puts it on the 'roo, and hands me his camera. When I take the picture and the flash goes off, so does the kangaroo. He must have been stunned—now it's our turn. We chase him, but he's too fast for us."

"That's a shame. So he lost his jacket?"

"Not just his jacket. That blasted animal has his passport, his wallet, his credit cards, his Olympic credentials. We'll have to spend tomorrow at the Embassy."

Upon hearing the story, Irv added, "Well, if I see a well-dressed kangaroo in Miami, I'll know he put the passport to good use."

Margie and the all-female U.S. Equestrian Team had different problems. Steve faithfully put his new laptop computer to good use and kept us informed almost daily via e-mail. He wrote us that, in spite of the Team's best efforts, they couldn't reach their expectations. Rhythmical, who was the most experienced horse on the U.S. Team, and Nona Garson fell on a slippery course the first day of competition, and were never able to recover fully. The show jumpers came in sixth in the Nations' Cup; but Margie, as well as Lauren Hough on Clasiko, and Laura Kraut on Liberty qualified for the Individual Finals.

We enjoyed Steve's e-mail about Margie's excitement in posing with President Clinton's daughter, Chelsea, and meeting Venus and Serena Williams. Most of her days were spent waiting for her turn in the practice ring; but Steve, along with the other spouses, managed to see some of the sights and climb in the Blue Mountains. His days also were filled with various chores. Even though he was not the official veterinarian for the U.S. horses, the riders wanted him to keep their horses in tip-top shape and he happily assisted.

I saved his last two messages, which read as follows:

"09/30/2000 7:17:34 AM Eastern Daylight Time

Hi, it's us again,

We went into Sydney last night and had dinner with Mike (Polaski), his entourage, and Jane (Forbes) Clark at a place called 'Catalina.' It was right on the bay and had great food. When we came out of the restaurant, there were bats flying all about—big bats! We then drove down to Hyde Park where we had a great view of Sydney and the Opera House which continually changed colors as we watched. There was a laser show so to speak from the tower in town. Sydney was just spectacular at night. The view of the bridge, lit up with the Olympic rings—really beautiful—along with all the glamorous yachts cruising the harbor, made for an unbelievable evening.

We hung at the barn today, because they had to jog this afternoon for tomorrow's event. I was going to go back in to see the Track and Field events tonight, but just ran out of steam.

Big day tomorrow, so it was probably better that I called it a day earlier than I had planned. I'll let you know how things go as soon as a get back tomorrow night. We aren't going to the closing ceremonies—too crowded—so we should be back at a decent hour to get packed. Talk to you soon. We love you all.

S&M"

"10/1/2000 2:34:33 AM Eastern Daylight Time

It was quite the finish. There were no clean rounds when Margie entered the ring (she was 22nd to go). She rode the course magnificently— over the water, through the combinations, every step rub free but had the last rail down—barely. The crowd roared in anticipation of the clear round and then let out a huge moan as the rail came down. It was a spectacular round. The second round, the wind was really kicking up. I don't know that this contributed to anything, but she ended up with 8 faults giving her a total of 12 leaving her in 10th place. She was leading American (and leading female) rider and we can all be proud of her performance. There were no double clean rounds so there was a 4-way jump off. Rodrigo Pessoa was the last to jump and would have to go clean to contend for the gold medal. It was unbelievable—he had the first jump down and then stopped out at the combination. No medal for him. Is this a tough sport or what? In fact, none of those that medalled in the Nation's Cup competition medalled here.

This is the last communiqué from Sydney. I hope this kept everybody feeling well informed. We're looking forward to getting home and seeing you all again.

G'day and G'bye from Sydney,

S&M"

Overall the U.S. riders fared well with Bronze Medals for eventing and dressage and a record-setting Individual Gold Medal in the three-day event as well. Because of the seventeen-hour difference in time, we knew the results before the events were shown or written about in the United States.

When Margie called before they left Sydney, we thanked her for providing us with the thrill of a lifetime. "And we're following your advice, Honey."

"What advice did I give you?"

"Enjoy the good times. This sport has so many ups and downs, you have to take your pleasure when you can." We greeted her upon her return. "You must feel so proud, Margie."

She responded. "I was thrilled. The whole thing was just so exciting...." She paused for a deep breath and then continued. "But I can hardly wait until the next time!"

*   *   *

Afterword

Irv and I look at our daughter. We know about all the obstacles. We know about all the injuries, past and present. We know how hard it was for her when she was growing up with no horse of her own, working in the kennels for extra lessons. We watched her find extra time, plan and juggle her schedule when other priorities made her riding dreams seem impossible. We know how difficult it was to be a "catch rider" when she was trying to work her way up to the "A" circuit, willing to try *any* horse just for the opportunity to compete. We empathized when professionals tried to dissuade her from show jumping because of her small stature and lack of financial backing. We worried about her the entire time she was a staff of one, driving a truck down mountains that made sure the weight of the horse trailers behind her pushed them to unwanted speeds.

Yes, there were many obstacles—on and *off* the course. But, for Margie Goldstein Engle, no hurdle was too high!

Appendix

Margie's Milestones

1986: Margie's first Grand Prix win (in Cincinnati on Daydream)
Leading Rider at Madison Square Garden (Open Jumper
Division)
Three Grand Prix wins total

1987: Three Grand Prix wins

1988: Margie's first World Cup competition in Gothenberg
(Places fourth in Grand Prix at World Cup)
Two Grand Prix wins

1989: Rider of the Year
Saluut II wins AHSA Horse of Year
Leading Rider American Gold Cup and American Jumping
Derby
Four Grand Prix wins

1990: While still using crutches off the course, wins 5 top-three plac-
ings in Grand
Prix events
Margie and Daydream win Washington International Puissance
(third time),
Madison Square Garden Puissance, and Toronto Puissance
Three Grand Prix wins

1991: Six Grand Prix wins plus numerous placings
Places four horses in a single Grand Prix competition
Wins Attitash Equine Festival for second year in a row

AGA Rider of the Year

AHSA/Hertz Rider of the Year

1992: Rides with brace (3 broken ribs, 5 crushed ribs)—Wins Rolex/National

GrandPrix ((NGL) Rider of the Year

Places four horses in a single Grand Prix event

Four Grand Prix wins

1993: Rolex/NGL Rider of the Year

First Rider ever to place first, second, third, fourth, and fifth in a single

Grand Prix class (Rolex Music City, in Nashville)

Five Grand Prix wins

1994: Most AGA wins (5) with the same horse in the same season (Saluut II)

Most Grand Prix wins (8) with the same horse (Saluut II), same season

Most Grand Prix wins (13) in a single season (Tampa Grandprix, WEF Challenge Series Final in Fla., Music City Grand Prix in Tenn., Las Colinas Grand Prix in Texas, Germantown Grand Prix in Pa., Upperville Jumper Classic in Va., Town & Country Motor City in Mich., North American Grandprix of Detroit, Miller's Harness Company in New York, Vermont Summer Grandprix, Turfway Park Grand Prix of Kentucky, Columbia Classic Benefit of Maryland, Grand Prix of Delaware)

Won World Cup Class in Port Jervis, N.Y. $100,000 Grand Prix

Two Grand Prix wins in two days (Germantown and Upperville)

First Rider to place six horses in the ribbons in a single Grand-Prix class

(Detroit)

Margie's total wins place her in the Millionaires' Club (along with Tim Grubb,
Hap Hansen, Rodney Jenkins, Leslie Lenehan, Michael Matz, and Katie
Monahan Prudent)
AGA Rider of the Year
1995: Wins Motor City Grand Prix second year in a row
Wins Music City Grand Prix for third year in a row on same horse (Sabantianni)
Only Rider to place five horses in a single Grand Prix
Seven Grand Prix wins
AGA Rider of the Year
1996: Six Grand Prix wins
AGA/Budweiser Rider of the Year
Volvo World Cup
1997: Seven Grand Prix wins
USET Team: Nations Cup Winner, Rome
USET Team: Nations Cup Winner, St. Gallen, Switzerland
Leading International Rider in St. Gallen, Switzerland
USET Team: Nations Cup Second Place, Aachen, Germany
Leading Lady Rider in Aachen, Germany
Individual Grand Prix Winner in Rome aboard Hidden Creek's Laurel
Individual Grand Prix Winner in Arnhem, Netherlands on H. C.'s Alveretto
1998: Nine Grand Prix wins
USET Team: Nations Cup Winner, Madison Square Garden, on Alveretto
USET Team: Nations Cup Winner, Montreal, on H.C.'s Laurel
World Cup Finals in Helsinki, Finland—Second Place
1999: Eleven Grand Prix wins
USET Team Silver Medal Award, Pan Am Games, in

Winnepeg
Fulfils lifelong dream: Wins American Invitational Grand Prix
Leading AGA computer list for number of wins (Rider of the Year Award
For the Sixth Time)
2000: USET Representative at World Cup
Five Times World Cup Finalist
Leads Olympic Trials
Totals: Ninety-three Grand Prix career wins to date (thereby becoming The First Show Jumping Rider
to win $3 million in prize money)
All Time Leading Money Winner in United States
Most Grand Prix Wins in U.S. Rider History
As we go to press, Margie has just won her *seventh* AGA Rider of the Year Award for 2000-2001!

A Brief History of Show Jumping

Through crudely scratched cave drawings or child-like equine statues, early humans expressed their fascination with horses. Once they took pen to paper, historians gloried in the daring mounted escapes of fugitives fleeing from battle. When Oliver Cromwell and the Stuart Kings added Arabians into the British breeding program, English horses developed an amazing ability to gallop and jump at virtually any speed.

Great Britain increased the popularity of equestrian displays by exhibiting these beautiful animals in shows that were a mixture of music hall performances and riding school exhibitions. From the seventeenth to the nineteenth century, the French, with their passion for *Grand Prix* (the richest or greatest prize), developed a wealth of great horsemen who essentially evolved the principles of riding that are still used to this day. In the twentieth century, show jumping ranked right after soccer as the spectator sport of choice throughout Europe, Canada, and South America.

In 1906, Count Clarence von Rosen proposed to the International Olympic Committee (IOC) that equestrian sports be included permanently in the Games. By 1912, three equestrian events in Stockholm made their debut: dressage, show jumping, and three-day eventing. Sweden won the gold in show jumping that year, as well as in the Olympics of 1920 and 1924.

In the first Olympics featuring equestrian competitors, only eight countries competed. In the 1932 Los Angeles Olympics, one lone winner in the Individual Finals, Lt. Nishi from Japan, received a gold medal. No team was classified as all were eliminated. By 1944, a record entry of 99 riders from seventeen countries competed in the Paris Olympics. At the Sydney Olympics 2000, new regulations with even higher standards eliminated many of the countries from competing. Only nations who had won in international qualifiers were eligible. In show jumping alone, there were fourteen countries, as well as seventeen riders from other nations who had qualified on the basis of their individual scores.

The United States first presented a Grand Prix in 1965 in Cleveland. Over the years, a circuit of events has grown. From eight major events in the late sixties, the number of Grand Prixs grew steadily. There are over a hundred events presented yearly currently offering several million dollars in prize money. Spectators can gauge the difficulty of a Grand Prix course by the prize money involved. The larger the amount, the more challenges the riders face.

Interest in jumping has resulted in a tremendous increase in the number of private owners of pleasure horses. In the United States, there are an estimated twenty-seven million riders. Unlike in the past when the sport was thought to be only for wealthy gentlemen riders, participants come from all walks of life, with ages ranging from sixteen to sixty. Six-time Olympian and the first American to win an individual Gold Medal in show jumping (in Mexico in 1968), William C. Steinkraus, describes the sport as, "….a unique combination of beauty, variety, excitement, the participation of both sexes on equal terms, and the fascinating collaboration between animal and man in nature."

Show Jumping Divisions and Difficulties

Jumping divisions within the show jumper classes include Schooling, Children's, Juniors, Adults, Amateur-Owner, Preliminary, Intermediate, Modified, and Open. The last four divisions are classified based on the amount of money the horse has earned in a given time frame. Only amateur riders who own their horses can show Amateur-Owner Jumpers. Amateur riders can show Adult-Amateur, and they do not have to actually own the horse. Only riders under 18 years of age can show Junior and Children's Jumpers. Schooling Jumpers may be ridden by anyone.

Grand Prix Show Jumpers present the most skilled riders/horses within the sport. The arenas in which they compete are the products of talented course designers who are riders themselves and know how to increase the difficulty of the jumps, turns, and time demands. Although these courses may look like those at a lower division, the height and spread of the obstacles, the arrangement, as well as the combinations of the hurdles, are all set up to require the utmost ability from the competitors.

The challenge is simple and straightforward: approximately fifteen to twenty obstacles to a course. If a horse falls or downs any portion of an obstacle (fence) or if he fails to clear a water hazard, he receives penalty points, called faults. The horses and riders must negotiate the course at the correct angle, height, and speed to clear the fences or hazards clean (without faults). Each downed or unsuccessful hurdle results in four faults. If the horse refuses an obstacle, he can (as printed in the program or announced prior to the event) receive three faults plus ten seconds added to his time. Second refusal results in further penalties. A third refusal results in automatic elimination from competition.

The rider also must be aware of the clock and stay within the guidelines to avoid time faults, a quarter of a point for each second. Should there be several riders with clean rounds within the time limit, a jump-off will determine the top winners. Most of the time, they come back in the same order as they rode in the first round to compete on a shortened course within a shorter time limit.

For Open Show Jumping competition, the rider and horse jump order (Order of Go) is determined in a drawing before an event. Most riders prefer a jump order closer to the end, so they know what they'll have to do to improve upon the performance of those who have preceded them. When a rider has earned his way into an invitational type class, the jump order is based on reverse order of qualification. The rider in the lead would go last and the rider placing last would go first with all those in between placed accordingly.

Often an outstanding rider will compete on more than one horse during a Grand Prix. This requires extraordinary talent, because each horse has his own temperament and characteristics that require the rider to adjust accordingly. In the Olympics or in Invitational Classes, the rider usually is limited to the horse on which he or she has qualified.

Watching competitors at the top of their field is a joy for both sports fans and those who simply love horses for their grace, speed, and ability to work as one with their riders.

Made in the USA